Jesse G. Montea

RESTLESS REDNECKS

Roy F. Wood

# RESTLESS REDNECKS

## Gay Tales of the Changing South

**Grey Fox Press**
**San Francisco**

Manufactured in the United States of America.


Most of these stories were first published in *Blueboy, Fag Rag, First Hand, Gala Review, Gay Sunshine Journal, GPU News, Honcho, Mandate* and *Manifest*.

*Library of Congress Cataloging in Publication Data:*

Wood, Roy F.
    Restless rednecks.

        1. Homosexuality—Fiction.    2. Southern States—
Fiction.   I. Title.
PS3573.05965R4       1985       813'.54       84-25298
ISBN 0-912516-90-9 (pbk.)

Distributed by the Subterranean Company, P.O. Box 10233, Eugene, OR 97440

## DEDICATION

This one is for Charles, with deep affection.

# CONTENTS

Preface   ix

Next Time   3

The Night the Dykes Destroyed Dick's Bar   14

Baptism   22

Where Have All the Heroes Gone?   33

A Passionate Attachment   43

Transfiguration   60

The Shrine   68

The Man Who Followed His Heart   82

Nursing Papa   94

A Time for Honesty   103

The Man Who Stood in the Corner   113

A Picture of Rex   120

The Lure of the Sirens   129

The Visitation   139

Masters of the Ceremony   145

# Preface

When I began writing, short stories were near the bottom of the list of what I hoped to accomplish. A *book* was what I had in mind: a thick, erudite tome . . . something along the lines of a novel by Thomas Mann, Charles Dickens, Ayn Rand or Patrick White.

Unhappily, I discovered it takes a very long time to complete a full-length book, particularly if one has to hold down a job and is rather lazy into the bargain! And there comes a time when people who call themselves writers, or authors, are no longer content with collecting their manuscripts in a file cabinet — before long they yearn to be published.

So, reluctantly, I put aside the book I was working on in order to toss together some short stories, in the notion, mistaken, that writing short fiction was easy and could be quickly done. Naturally, I expected these efforts would be readily accepted and would soon flow into print.

None of the above turned out to be true.

The time, effort and, yes, enjoyment, which has gone into the creation of the stories in this collection have changed all my assumptions about short fiction. I now have a much deeper respect for those who have succeeded in this field and I read them today with far more insight than I did a few years ago.

*Restless Rednecks* grew out of my attempts to depict gay people in the South. I've lived most of my life in rural or small-town southern communities and I realize there is a considerable difference in the experiences one encounters in this environment, as compared with that of the urban areas. The most obvious is of course the nature of the sexhunt. In cities of any size numerous men are available and the pursuit is more relaxed. Rural byways have fewer males and one must use a greater degree of caution in cruising them. Nevertheless, as some of these stories illustrate, there are enough opportunities to make life in the country interesting.

Interesting? Maybe, you might say, but why "Rednecks"? In these stories rednecks are mostly men who are strong, virile, earthy: true sons of the earth. They exude male sexuality and aren't bigoted about how they obtain release. Such studs do exist . . . truly! Because they consider themselves primarily hetero, they don't get involved in the games gays often play with each other. Rednecks are very direct as, I hope, they are in the stories about them. At the same time, there are less pleasant aspects of country life: witness Fat Freddy among others.

Let me hasten to reassure everyone, however, that these stories are indeed "fiction." Some, of course, are based on tiny kernels of truth. "Transfiguration," for example, stems from my personal experience with, and devotion to, bodybuilding. I started lifting about four years ago, and the mental transformation, *for me*, is pretty much that experienced by my protagonist. And yes, I did run across a muscleman poster which I still have (any bodybuilders out there want to compare artwork?). The rest of the story, unhappily, is pure fiction—or wishful thinking if you will.

If you've lived very long in the South, especially outside of large cities, you've likely experienced a "Visitation." Here, I needed very little imagination to move from reality to story line—very little imagination indeed! And I'm fortunate in that my imagination can see an erotic scenario in almost every aspect of daily life. At the same time, given the cónservative nature of this region and the times in general, unavoidable sublimation can lead to exciting fantasy, the exploration of possibilities of what might be.

Yet, in spite of the great pleasure I as a writer get from my work, it is my firm conviction that an author of fiction, especially short fiction, has an obligation to tell a story. And that is what I've tried to do here. Some of the stories are designed to be read with one hand, others to make you laugh or at least smile; and some tell a tale which might make you reflect for a few moments. They should, all in all, make you feel good about being a gay man! And I hope they give you pleasure in the reading.

Roy F. Wood
Athens, Georgia 1984

RESTLESS REDNECKS

# Next Time . . .

The South has many famous cities—Atlanta, Miami, New Orleans, to name just a few. These metropolises are unmistakably southern in atmosphere; yet for every area which has gained enough souls to claim the designation "city," there are a thousand others too small even to be labeled towns. These are where the remnants of the real South may yet be found. No area is so typical of this rural pastoralism than the section of Georgia south of Macon. Here lies a large portion of the state, almost half, where cities cease to exist and towns become hard to find. A couple of places—Valdosta, Albany—aspire to cityhood; but they fall short of their goal.

This area of Georgia consists of scrub oak hillsides and deep pine forests, interlaced with myriad tilled fields. The mile after mile of cornfields, and lately soybeans, which has replaced the age-old king cotton, all exude a magnetism of their own. The countryside, for all its countless faults, still possesses a mystical power, capable of holding certain of her sons in bondage. Such men, if no longer exactly bound to the soil, are still eternally ensnared by something—a scent from the woodland or the shrill cry of a nightbird, unhearable farther north. The shimmering sticky hotness of long, lazy summer afternoons, autumn changes, winter's dull drab grayness, unrelieved by snow. The rebirth of spring. These all combine to weave a mysterious and tangled web, binding victims in invisible chains to the region, to the land. Many cannot will themselves away.

*Next Time . . .*

Such a person was David Benson. The man, thirty, was tall, lean, deeply tanned; his face too long for his frame, his nose too small. Deep-set coal-black eyes redeemed the head; his mouth gave a hint of an exasperating sensual quality. His face ended in a square-set jutting jawline of moderate attractiveness.

Benson was born to the area, raised on a small homestead. Not a farm, yet surrounded by all the accoutrements of farm life. His parents had been gentle folk. They had raised their only child differently from his peers — how differently, he was thankful they never learned. Prudent management sent him north to the state university. There Benson found many things he liked, some he needed; few he could not live without. He trekked back south after graduation, having learned enough to know he should leave the area; yet still in love with the land, his covenant with it solid and intact.

He worked in real estate, which kept him outdoors a fair amount of time and provided a suitable salary. In an area where marriage was the norm, he anticipated trouble because of his single state — but even here the natives were slowly, surely, changing. That new god of the dark night, television, homogenized its worshipers even in the remote byways of south Georgia. The neighbors still gossiped incessantly. They craned their necks at every vehicle which roared past their windows, fearful of missing the latest news, yet succumbing, gradually, to the notion that their neighbor's business was his alone, open to their criticism, but not always to change.

Settling in, Benson stayed to himself. He adored the homeplace, his alone now, where there was always something to be done. Especially early Saturday mornings when the sun created mists of dew and birds seemed louder than an open-air band and when the air was crisp like an old timey starched shirt, before the sweat of the day melted it to limpness. They were days of energetic work, done to his own purpose.

Yet, as time passed, Benson's very efficiency left few chores still to be done. Or the skies would pour forth their leaden loads and leave him helpless to keep the hours occupied.

Those days, worst of times! He could be pushed by them into

traveling northward to Atlanta, or south to Jacksonville, to haunts he knew of—but he never found in them the happiness he sought—only momentary solace from a vast emptiness which threatened, at times, to engulf him.

Intellectually he loved the men he found there. His physical desires for them did not result in his feeling shame or guilt over that aspect of his personality. He regretted only that he could not be happy in the cities where others like him lived. Nor, he was forced to admit, did the plastic, brittle "good-looks" everyone strived for, impress him overmuch. Men who looked as if they feared a drop of sweat, honestly gained, as most people would a deadly snake. Benson could not wholly enjoy his excursions into their cities because he knew most men there would not accept his farm—would find the soil degrading, not warm and arousing—nor would they pause long enough to notice the first breaking buds of March and April. In so many ways, he did not fit in. Not in the city, not in the rural niche of his own life. Each trip he made to the monsters of concrete, Benson vowed would be the last; he lashed himself for physical weakness, yet, finally, knowingly, he would drive to them again, seeking a phantom which existed, he supposed, only in his mind.

In his own realm, towns did exist—people lived—and while fearful of exposing a nature he knew unacceptable to his neighbors, he would sometimes, even close to home, set out in his own elusive way, seeking the attainment of dream and desire.

On these occasions Benson reluctantly ventured into one of the towns closest to his home, Tilton. This community one day found itself on the site of an interstate highway and had decided, sullenly, to grow and prosper. For Benson, who lived thirty minutes from the area, the situation was not without possibilities. He could visit the bars of large motel chains and, if he were lucky, meet someone with whom to spend some time. These episodes, usually quickly over and sooner forgotten, were more a product of physical necessity than anything else. He found them often sordid, rarely satisfying and never permanent.

Late one summer afternoon, evening actually, he returned home from an especially profitable day at the office. Grabbing a beer from the kitchen, he padded barefoot out to the front porch. He dropped down into the old-fashioned porch swing, drinking his beer and listening to the late afternoon sounds, feeling lazy, relaxed, at peace with himself and his world. A car drove by, raising a storm of dust. The sun sank into a bank of clouds, sending forth long beams of strangely-rayed light. His mood, as it was wont to do, shifted slowly, settling into a mild despondency as the golden ball of sun disappeared in the west. If only the chair opposite him were filled! If he could see there another man . . . Disgusted with himself, he put down the empty can and went to perform the evening chores.

Twilight deepened and night sounds slowly came to the fore. Crickets, frogs by the pond, bats circling overhead; suddenly Benson decided this night he would not sit home. He would go into town, have a couple of drinks and see who, if anyone, was about. Maybe tonight . . . maybe this time . . .

His drive into town saw dusk deepen to darkness. Real night arrived and the oppressive heat slowly began to loosen its grip on the region. Benson thought about where to go for the evening. The motel bars held no appeal. He knew what he would find there. Yet the town offered nothing else. There was one small hole in the wall, not far from the superhighway. He'd been there once, finding it generally insipid; country music out of a radio, a battered whore trying to pick up whomever she could—no sense going there again. He stopped at a traffic light, however, and noted the little place two blocks ahead of him. On the spur of the moment he decided to gamble on it—for a short while at least.

Every time Benson entered such a place, his stomach muscles tightened—not from fear, as much as from the need to throw up caution signs for himself. Remember to nod at the women, don't look too long at the men, don't, whatever you do, make a wrong move nor do anything which might signal your desire to someone unreceptive. The restrictions annoyed him, reminding him that the only good feature about traveling to the cities was being able to visit places where the need for such mental reservations did not exist.

Mentally prepared, he pushed open the dingy door and entered the poorly-lit room.

The bar was almost empty. A fat, greasy-looking bartender leaned behind the long counter. His hair was spidery, oiled and rapidly disappearing over a jowly face. He glanced up, with no smile of welcome, as Benson came toward him.

"What'll ya have?" he questioned tiredly. Not caring and not minding that his disinterest showed.

Benson gave his order and paid his money. The transaction was complete.

There were only two other customers in the place. A man and woman sat at the bar; he was overweight, bleary-eyed and drunk. The female next to him was a flighty blonde wearing a too-tight blouse over breasts which threatened to upend her. She and the male were in animated conversation. Tammy Wynette was wafting forth from the jukebox, an addition since the last time Benson had visited the dim hole. He took his beer and went to one of the booths in the rear, from which he could see the entire bar.

The scene did not depress Benson; he'd known what to expect before he entered—it simply caused a feeling of melancholia to spread over him, which, when all was said and done, was as good a depressant as alcohol. He sipped beer, hoped the woman wouldn't turn her attention towards him, and allowed his thoughts to flow limpidly through his mind like syrup poured on a cold morning.

He sat, drank, expected nothing. Time crawled by—or raced; either way he paid no mind to the minutes as they played with eternity. He put his hand around the can to raise it once more to his lips when the door swung open—admitting only another couple, of indeterminate age, with the silly-grin look of those who had already drunk too much.

A quarter of an hour later he was on his second can, mentally preparing to leave, yet trying to force himself to stay away from the interstate strip. Go home, was his advice to himself. Deep in a momentary daydream, he missed hearing the door open. His eye caught a movement and he stared at the newcomer with eyes which widened quickly in astonishment as he appraised the man now at the bar.

He was tall—as tall as Benson, but with more flesh on his bones. Not fat, though; firmness showed even from a distance: short cropped brown hair, a nearly square face, good-looking in an athletic sense of the word. Browned deeply, he was obviously an outdoor worker of some sort. Benson immediately broke all the commandments he had given to himself by looking overlong at the man. No harm was done, however, as the stranger was ordering a drink and the other occupants of the bar were too busy with their own affairs to notice even if light had permitted. The man took his beer and looked around, openly scornful of the people in the room; his glance took in Benson. The scornful look changed to one of appraisal and puzzlement. His eyes did not linger, nor did they hint, only studied briefly before their owner moved to the end of the bar, to the right of Benson. The two men could observe each other with ease if they were of a mind to do so. Benson dared not let his eyes follow the form. He could not say at what the other was looking.

A spasm of emotion racked Benson. This, after all, was what he'd hoped would happen. He'd wanted a man like this new-comer to enter the bar—but he felt hopelessly inept when one did appear. In a town like Tilton, in a bar such as this one, there was no chance anything would happen. At least, nothing along the lines of his desire.

He stole a careful glance to his right. The attractiveness of the other moved him. If he could only suggest he *approved* of such a man—yet his approval would mean nothing and his admiration, were it known, would be scorned and despised. Resentment welled up in him and as quickly subsided. He could not blame people for their prejudices—only regret that they hated without reason. The other man spoke to no one, made no moves of any kind. Gradually Benson slipped back into his own reverie.

Uneasily he felt the eyes of the stranger touch him. He looked up and their eyes met, locked for an instant. Benson was about to avert his glance when the man nodded at him. The motion was slowly done—exaggerated almost (but not quite) to the point of scorn. Puzzled by the move, Benson gazed openly at the other, who after a time unhurriedly turned away. Then, carelessly, casually, the man left the end of the bar where he had seated himself and walked to the point where the old man behind the bar was selling beverages. He bought another drink and leisurely moved back towards where he had been.

At first, Benson thought the guy was leaving. Remorse seeped into him. Another opportunity missed, he told himself, but knew there had been no opportunity and nothing missed. Then he saw the man buy his drink, saw him returning . . .

Benson, aware he ought not in any way notice the man, who, since they had already glanced at one another once, would think it unusual and peculiar if he looked again, could in no way help himself. He stared frankly and openly at the man.

The other, seeing the look, appeared almost to grow taller, more handsome; Benson, with sudden sharp foreboding, turned away. The spell was broken. The stranger continued towards his spot at the end of the bar, when abruptly he stopped, shifted his weight and in a second was standing at Benson's booth.

"Mind if I join you?" he asked.

Benson was thankful for the dim light. He felt his face go through many shades of color but having gotten himself into an unpredictable situation, he wanted above all to measure up to his own expectations.

"Not at all," he replied with, he hoped, the proper tone of nonchalant interest.

"Dull in here tonight," Benson added, to keep the conversation going.

"Always is," agreed the other. He took a drink of his beer and offered his hand. A firm, hard, rugged hand which sent a charge through Benson as he gripped it.

"Name's Dan Taylor," his companion said by way of introduction. "Live over on 82, north of Nashville."

"Dave Benson." He gave the pertinent information. Was it his imagination or did they shake hands a fraction of a second longer than necessary?

They talked a few minutes about inconsequential matters.

Next Time . . .

Benson, trying valiantly to control his emotions as well as his expectations, was surprised to hear the man in front of him lived not far from his own small holdings. Benson suspected Dan must have moved into the area while he'd been away at school a few years back.

Their conversation progressed well. This fact alone amazed Benson, who in similar situations usually found he had no words to utter. The hardest part of evenings like this was attempting to "make" conversation. Dan, however, was talkative. As the first few minutes passed, Benson suddenly sensed his acquaintance was nervous. The words the other spoke, had Benson been a friend of Taylor's, would have seemed forced, artificial.

In a slack moment, when Taylor looked away into another corner of the bar, Benson eagerly observed the man. He felt his own body tighten with joy at the physical presence of Dan Taylor. The man was attractive—his existence across the table a dilemma. Benson was caught up in the conflicts of emotional turmoil. He was pleased being this close to Taylor. Yet he wanted more. He wished he had the nerve to bring his leg into contact with Taylor's beneath the table. He was fearful—they were almost neighbors! He dared not risk an overt move. Even as he thought the words, Taylor's attention returned, and—was there not a brief touch against Benson's knee? No. He couldn't be sure. Fool! Benson promptly roused himself to reality, while his spirit tossed in agony.

Taylor meanwhile finished his drink. He smashed and bent the can in capable hands, sighed and said, "I wouldn't mind a couple more beers, but I don't think much of this joint. You got any favorite places around here?"

"No," answered Benson truthfully. "There aren't any others except the motel bars on the interstate. I don't care for them, much."

"Me neither."

A brief silence. Benson sensed he should say something befor the pause became too long and broke the new-found relationship. Silence among friends was fine—between new acquaintances, deadly. He forced himself to speak, "Were you wantin' to drink, or were you lookin' for a spot with entertainment?"

Taylor chuckled. "Mostly, I wanted a few beers and a chance to get out of the house. I like livin' by myself, but . . ." His voice trailed off, leaving the sentence unfinished.

Benson, to his astonishment and embarrassment, found himself saying, ". . . I've got plenty of beer back at my place. It's right on your way home, not out of the way . . ." The offer, miraculously, was accepted. Such a small exchange to be so brimming with expectations.

The journey to his house was a ride of great trepidation for Benson. Taylor followed behind in his own vehicle, allowing Benson plenty of time to ponder his foolishness. He wanted desperately to reach out and touch this man, hold him, be held by him—they seemed to have so much in common. But he knew he must in no way say or do anything which would hint at what he felt. He was very surprised Taylor had agreed to return with him. Such an acceptance was unusual—most men would have preferred staying in town where they might have a chance of meeting a woman. Did he dare hope? Bitterly, Benson pushed hope from the ledge of his mind. For such as himself, there could be no hope. *Anticipation* was all he might dream of—he knew full well the community's attitudes towards people like him. The icy fury he felt at both himself for his fearfulness, and the others for their views, helped bring him closer to reality. By the time he pulled into his driveway, his ardor had cooled considerably, and Benson was mentally kicking himself for inviting this stranger into his home.

Taylor in his living room changed all that. Benson brought drinks, put music on his sound system and they sat down. Benson on the sofa, Taylor in a large chair next to it. A small lamp's rays shone pale and inadequately about the room. Taylor's visible flesh—his face, arms, hands—gleamed bronze in the dim visibility of the room. Benson felt resolve fleeing. If *only* he could find out whether or not his visitor had any idea what was in his mind. That he managed to keep a conversation going at all was a minor miracle. They finished the first beers, Benson went

Next Time . . .

for two more. Returned. Taylor was up now, walking around the
room, looking at the books, restless. Was he sorry he'd come,
Benson wondered. Or was he full of the same sweet-bitter un-
certainties as Benson? They both ended up sitting on the sofa.
Not too close, not yet . . .

Benson, aching to reach out and touch the man, held back.
The fear, the pain instilled in countless ways over a lifetime was
sufficient to conquer his hope for happiness. And suddenly he
realized Taylor could very probably make him happy. Even with
all the beer he'd drunk in the course of the evening, the excru-
ciating desire within him to grasp Taylor, feel the man in his
arms and to be touched himself, all stood for nothing compared
to the throbbing waves of pain and hopelessness which flooded
him at the thought the man might reject such admiration. Benson did not fear rejection of his body, nor rejection of himself as
Benson, although he was never pleased by either—but he could
not face rejection of his ideal of love. He knew that the feelings
he had for Taylor, were they allowed to grow, flower and
mature, would produce beauty beyond all he'd ever known.
Trembling, he sat on the sofa and dared not take the gamble.

Taylor, as they drank, grew restive again. Benson imagined
the man moved ever so much closer to him. Taylor's shoulders
grew wider, his charm more magnetic, drawing Benson closer
and closer to him. It became more difficult not to give in to
Taylor's pull. Fear of condemnation battled with hope of happiness and both combatants tottered on a precipice, neither winning—yet. The minutes dragged by—unspeakable agonies for
Benson. Taylor finally began looking as if he must leave. Instead,
one last time he sat down, this time so close to Benson their legs
brushed together. Taylor had found a book to question Benson
about—that was the excuse for the closeness, a closeness which
was brief, momentary; a fleeting glimpse of time standing still.

Taylor got up to put the book away. Benson, in that instant
knew his fear had defeated him. He suddenly realized with a
clarity he could not understand that as he, in fear, had dared
make no overt moves, so Taylor, by his very moves about the
room, by his restless manner, had been trying to communicate a

message of his own desires to Benson.

Taylor now moved back to the chair. Unsure, puzzled, fearful himself of pursuing a quarry he believed beyond reach. He stood up. The evening was ending. As they said good-bye, however, Taylor looked hard into Benson's eyes, "If you're not busy, stop by my place Saturday."

He was gone.

As the sound of Taylor's truck evaporated into the cooled night air, Benson stood alone. His eyes did not see the moon which scurried back and forth behind clouds as if playing hide and seek.

Benson saw only the form of Taylor. Masculine strength, manly beauty which he could have shared tonight had he not feared so much. Next time . . . He shook himself and went back toward the house. Saturday seemed an eternity away. If only *tonight* he had overcome . . . he damned himself, but even more he berated the disquietude which had stopped his actions. When he met Taylor on Saturday, as he vowed he would, things would end differently. Next time he would overcome the uneasiness, the apprehensions that others forced into his consciousness. Next time he would seize the initiative and seek happiness no matter what came of it. Oh yes, next time the ending would be different he promised himself as he entered the empty house. Next time . . .

# The Night the Dykes Destroyed Dick's Bar

I was in attendance the night four dykes destroyed Dick's Bar.
The name of the joint wasn't *really* Dick's Bar—it was chris-
tened the Hilltop Lounge. Enterprising architects, however,
shaped the building to resemble a cock and balls, hence the
name change. You couldn't tell much about the bar's design
from ground level—which is how everyone involved got away
with it—but from the air it . . . stood out, so to speak. Dick's Bar
was one of the most famous landmarks in South Georgia.

The clientele, for the most part, were would-be cowboys and
lean, bronzed farmhands. Redneck, rowdy, mean as hell, ready
for a fight anytime. You might wonder what the hell *I* was doing
in such a place.

Well, when you live over a hundred miles from any city, love
making it with guys and are horny all the time, you got two
choices: stay home and jerk off or take your chances cruising
places like Dick's Bar.

I admit it wouldn't be safe for most gay men. You gotta have
balls *and* bulk to try making pickups in the Dick's Bars of the
South. And, without bragging, I reckon I can say I got both. I'm
six-feet-three, two hundred pounds of solid muscle—and I've
got the enviable reputation of being able to handle myself in a
fight. The fact I prefer guys is generally known—and the closer
it gets to closing time, the better I look to some of these ramy
studs. I'll give head if that's what they want, but I love letting
some hung, hot dude work on my ass with at least an eight-inch

rod. That sort of news travels; so some nights I score. When I don't, the ambience of the bar makes the visit worthwhile.

The last night of the bar's life started off like most others. I drove into the half-filled parking lot in my pickup around nine-thirty (farmers start partying earlier than city folks). The way the place was set up, you entered at the tip of the cock. Inside, there was a long bar, the entire length of one side of the building. The other wall had booths. The "balls" section contained a small stage for live bands, the johns, and a couple of spots where you could lean against the walls. I liked that area best. Everybody made a few trips to the john and you could see who might be available. Most nights there were twice as many men as women in the place. Guys with women generally sat in the booths where they could make out in the dim light.

I stopped at the bar and got me a beer. The bartender was civil; I nodded at a couple of people I knew, got ignored by one asshole I'd given a blow-job several weeks previously and was acknowledged by a couple of others who'd screwed me in the past. They weren't above a repeat performance and I wouldn't have minded myself—both were hot and hung—but I had other plans for the evening.

The band they were showcasing had played at several beer joints in the neighborhood. I had my eye on the pianoplayer. He possessed a neat body, soft-looking brown hair and a puppydog face that almost blushed every time I caught his glance. His biggest selling point was the box he showed. His cock seemed to hang down his left leg halfway to his knee. I was panting to see if it were real—and to find out how big it grew when excited.

The band hadn't set up yet, so I found a good spot back by the bandstand and got comfortable. Across the way I noticed Sally the Sucker had set up shop.

Sally was a hoot! In spite of the fact she was competition, I liked her. From time to time she'd slip into the men's john, install herself on one of the thrones and peer through the cracks between the stalls until she saw something she liked, then she'd make a proposition.

"How's tricks, Sally?" I asked as she came over.

"Lousy! These guys ain't got no *stamina*! The last two I tried giving head said they had to save it for their girlfriends. Bastards that can't get it up twice a night ain't worth much! How you been doing?"

"Not bad. Got Jim Thompson over to my place three nights ago for a session."

"I'll be damned! He as big as we've heard?"

"No. About nine. A short nine at that, but he fucks like hell— best I've had for weeks."

Sally sighed. "Some people have all the luck," she said. "Who you after tonight? That damned pee-anner player?"

"Yeah," I answered. "We still competing?"

"Damn right! I want that meat myself!"

We laughed, talked about the possibilities of Greg, the piano-player, and watched the place start filling up.

Sally bummed the price of a beer off me—her reputation's worse than mine, strangely enough, and the management expects her to spend more money than someone who might be there simply to spend an evening getting drunk.

While she was gone, I saw this stud in a cowboy hat head towards the john. I followed him.

He was at one of the pisspots so I went to the one next to him and pulled out my cock. The damn thing was half-hard which was both good and bad. My neighbor was no fool. He stared at me intently, meanly, finally saying, "Lookin' at a guy that way might lead to me thinkin' you was interested."

"You might be right," I replied, staring at him, openly, arrogantly.

He didn't like that.

"Why the fuck should I want to fool around with a fag when I got a hot pussy waiting for me?"

"Because my ass is tighter than her pussy," I told him, "and I know more about what guys like than a woman could ever learn. Give it a try, cowboy."

He wasn't having any. At least not at the moment.

"I oughtta knock the hell outta you."

"I'd be careful of that if I were you," I cautioned him. "A

simple 'no' is good enough. Hell, if you aren't interested, others will be."

He shrugged disdainfully, stuffed his cock back in his pants and zipped up—with some difficulty since he'd started getting hard. He left hurriedly, embarrassed, I think, because his meat was interested even if he professed not to be.

After a minute, I followed him out of the john.

The band had arrived and was tuning up.

Greg saw me right off—and I swear he blushed. Damn! He was poured into his levis and that cock of his was outlined like an outdoor billboard! He got me so hot I had to look away. It was time for another beer anyway.

I leaned on the bar and got the bartender's attention. He knows what I drink, and I always tip, so he brought me a can of brew. I was turning to go back and cruise Greg when I noticed these four women who'd just entered the place.

One of 'em was real pretty—had long black hair and looked a little bit like Crystal Gayle, who isn't bad looking—for a woman. The others, however, were three of the biggest, meanest-looking dykes I've ever seen. Naturally, I've got nothing against lesbians— except for the fact they have no sense of humor—but I don't like it much when lesbians or gay men work overtime to fit all the stereotypes so perfectly. These three could have been proto-types for the term "diesel dykes." I admit I was curious as to what they were doing in a place like Dick's Bar.

Well, none of *my* business. At least *they* wouldn't be com-petition!

Just as I turned to leave, however, the madness commenced.

A drunk cowboy approached the Crystal Gayle lookalike. The more he tried detaching her from her companions, the more she pressed herself against Big Momma.

The cowboy persisted.

Big Momma soon had enough.

"That'll do, fella. Back off!"

"Don't see nobody who'll *make* me," he sneered, reaching for "Crystal's" long, dark hair.

Big Momma's hamlike arm stopped him midway. She spun

him around, pulled his offending hand up behind his back, kicked him in the ass and sent him sprawling, face down, onto the floor.

The regulars didn't take to that. They didn't like the women, nor were they happy at seeing a guy manhandled so easily. Two or three stepped forward to "help out."

It was the beginning of a free-for-all.

The three dykelike women placed "Crystal" in their midst, turned their backs to her and took on the bar. Big Momma jerked the now-kneeling cowboy to his feet, lifted him off the floor and literally threw him into his companions. She then picked up a chair and broke it over the head of another rangy stud, sending him reeling and howling in agony. Women in the booths started screaming—and alternately giggling—and a few fled as more cowboys tried subduing the dykes, without any success. They were smart fighters and, with their defensive arrangement, were more than a match for drunk men.

I decided I'd better head back to the rear of the place. There was a door back by the bandstand, plus a couple of windows if things got hectic.

By this time most of the patrons were either involved in the brawl or were egging on those who were. Bottles started flying around; the band members were shouting, trying to save both themselves and their instruments.

Over in a corner, Sally had her head in some guy's crotch, sucking away, oblivious to everything going on around her. So was the guy.

I ducked a beer can, still half-full, and tumbled into the last booth. Right across from me was the cowboy I'd propositioned in the john. He grinned at me this time, suddenly friendly.

"They're gonna wreck this goddamned joint." The prospect seemed to please him. "You still interested?" he asked me in a quick change of direction.

"I might be," I said, cautious all of a sudden. "What happened to your pussy?"

"She didn't want to put out, so I tole her 'bout your offer." He laughed in the dimness. "That pissed her off. She said if'n

I was that horny I could have you."

My hand crept under the table to his leg. Through his levis I could feel his cock starting to stiffen. I was about to commit myself and leave Greg for another night when somebody hit Cowboy over the head with a chair leg. It was a waste since the guy wasn't doing anything. I ducked down and stayed conscious. Under the table I contemplated unzipping Cowboy's pants to see what he had but figured I'd do better getting back to the door in case escape became more important than cock-hunting.

By now the whole front section of the bar was a shambles. The dykes were still standing and swinging away. They appeared to be slowly working their way towards the front door. It was obvious that by the time they reached it, no one else would be on his feet.

The band members, meanwhile, had grabbed their instruments and fled, leaving Greg crouched behind his piano, wondering forlornly what to do. Sally, the opportunistic bitch, having finished one man, was pulling herself onto the stage and racing for Greg. I leaped onto the platform, grabbed Sally in my arms, opened the back door and deposited her outside.

"The joint's on fire," I hissed in her ear.

"Like hell it is," she hollered. "That ain't fair!"

"In this business, everything you can get away with is fair," I reminded her as I swiftly ducked inside and latched the door so she couldn't come back indoors. With her one-track mind, I probably saved her life.

Having gotten Sally out of the way, I joined Greg behind the piano. The turmoil was now spilling back into the "balls" of the bar. Pieces of broken chairs and other debris were flying over the piano and dropping at our feet.

"Messy, ain't it, Greg?"

He looked unhappy. Maybe it was my hand feeling up that splendid cock of his—which through his pants felt every inch as real as it looked.

"Hey fella—I gotta get outta here."

"Fine with me. Let's go to my place!"

"I better not . . ."

"Hell, you feel ready . . ."

"What . . . you want me to do?" His hesitant question delayed a decision.

"We'll do whatever you want," I assured him, "nothing more. But I'd love you to bang my ass with that big cock of yours."

He stared at me. In the fragmentary light I could see disbelief written across his face.

"Everybody says I'm too big," he complained.

"I won't," I promised, hoping I'd be able to live up to my own advertising.

He temporized. "I don't know—I'm only supposed . . . to bang the piano."

"You sure 'bout that?"

"No . . . I ain't. Hell, you done gone and got me stiff. And keepin' your goddamn hand on my pecker ain't reducin' it none." He swallowed, his face looked frightened and interested all at the same time.

"Could you *really* take this dick up your ass?" he asked at last.

"I'll damn sure try—" I began.

We were interrupted by a small explosion up front. While we'd been talking somebody had started a fire and the flames, now out of control, had reached the small gas grill behind the bar. The blaze was rapidly heading our way.

Greg and I looked at each other.

"Let's *go*!" I said.

We rushed to the back door and let ourselves out.

Other people were pouring out of the front of the bar. I hoped somebody remembered to rescue that Cowboy.

(They did—I met him several weeks later and talked him into a trip back home with me.)

By the time the fire trucks arrived it was hopeless.

The dykes, still encircling "Crystal" like she was a princess, proudly got in their car and drove away. Everyone was so damn glad to see the last of them, nobody made any effort to detain them for the cops.

Greg and I sat in my truck for a few minutes watching the flames do their work. I kept my hand on his crotch, keeping that cock hard and ready. Finally I detached myself enough to crank up the truck and we drove to my place.

I was sure sorry to see Dick's Bar go up in smoke like that. Still, the night wasn't a total loss: I got the pianoplayer.

# Baptism

When he was six, Samuel Mathis got "runned over" by a school bus, and as far as he was concerned, this accident changed the rest of his life. Some children are said to be permanently affected by run-ins with dirty old men; for Samuel, it was the "Accident," and his resulting encounters with little old religious ladies.

Other problems arose as a direct result of Samuel's unfortunate mishap, though happily none of these was of a physical nature. Time spent in hospital and recuperating at home caused him to miss out on the initial phase of friendship-building among his peers. Consequently, he became an unpopular child. Admiration of him did not increase as he aged.

He blamed everything on the Accident.

A pattern was set while he was recovering at home. Those days, not pleasant, were marked by much attention and many gifts. The gifts included puzzles and books, all of which led to rapid increases in Samuel's mental abilities. By the time he returned to school, he was far ahead of his classmates, most of whom were never interested in developing their empty little minds.

The fact that substantial numbers of the books presented to Samuel were of a religious nature was an additional disaster. The bearers of these volumes selected them, no doubt, with the best of intentions, but they were diabolical little tracts—containing visions of hell capable of frightening the most hardened of sinners into at least a temporary repentance. They played "hell" with Samuel's precocious, imaginative mind. These "good works," in time, were to produce an uncomfortable harvest.

Along with their insidious gifts came an unremitting curiosity on the part of the simpering ladies who offered them. "Was the child 'damaged'?" they would ask breathlessly, rolling their eyes heavenward, as if expecting God, rather than the boy's mother, to boom back an answer.

The mother always generously revealed Samuel's naked limbs for the ladies' perusal—much as one might display links of sausages. Once the exhibition was over everyone shook their heads and murmured about "God's Will." Samuel was seldom addressed directly except at the beginning and end of each visit. The mother made veiled sexual references at which all tittered appreciatively. Six, after all, was far too young for any knowledge of SEX. Samuel hated the whole embarrassing business. Later, he traced his dislike of women to this period of his life.

Like most things, Samuel's tribulations eventually passed away. He returned to school and a "normal" life—except that it wasn't.

Samuel had too many strikes against him to ever be "normal" in the sense the word was used in South Georgia. He was too mentally advanced, his parents too poor; he could not establish rapport with anyone. Children of the wealthy avoided him, those of the poor did not understand him. Without friends, Samuel became absorbed with religion.

Religion both awed and frightened him. He often awoke, sweating and shivering at the same time, dreaming of himself in hell. The preachers he listened to had a better knack of presenting hell, terrible and foreboding, than in extolling the "joys" of heaven. Samuel considered himself a sinful child and the path to heaven appeared painful and uncertain. Nevertheless, he decided the goal was worth the effort. By becoming "religious," he was able to parade his superiority over other children. Samuel developed into an insufferable brat. Frowning at each "hell" and "damn" his mother uttered, refusing to have anything to do with the rough and tumble activities of boys his own age, he be-

lieved himself well on his way to that "beautiful land." He might
have continued on this disastrous path had not two things inter-
vened. The first was his habit of reading everything he could get
his hands on; the second was puberty.

Samuel's reading was indiscriminate. He read Tarzan books
for the splendid pictures of the loinclothed ape-man without
realizing why they appealed to him. He stole his mother's paper-
back of *Peyton Place* and read it voraciously, disgusted but fascinated. Then his own sex drive struck.

The advent of his sexual capability commenced a monumental
battle between Samuel and his Flesh. Discovering the rapture of
masturbating, he became a slave to the demon between his legs.
It was very distressing. The Mathis' were without indoor
"facilities," and their outhouse was a frequent abode for snakes,
seeking an escape from the hot Georgia summers. Samuel was
forever racing from the place, screaming for his father to come
and chase away bewildered serpents. The father, usually nap-
ping, was disgusted by his son's sissylike attitudes, and each
snake-in-the-outhouse episode brought about a confrontation
between father and son. Symbolically, it was a tableau of utter
perfection, but after each occurrence, Samuel was reduced to
tears and so failed to perceive the beauty of the situation.

Neither snakes, Jesus or anything else stayed Samuel's hand
from his groin. Long prayers, tearfully offered, and vivid recol-
lections of hell's terrible abyss became impotent soldiers in the
battle between Samuel and his body. The situation produced
such an emotional and psychological maelstrom in his mind that
a lesser youth would have been reduced to imbecility. In
Samuel's case, the inability to cease his sinful habit was, in the
long run, his "salvation."

For, as he grew towards maturity, Samuel struggled, in the
context of his experience, to reconcile his ideas about religion
and sex. He was doubly handicapped: having never been allowed
to preview the case for human freedom (much less, *sexual* freedom), he was mentally inhibited by years of exposure to doctrines which humiliated and degraded mankind. Samuel's struggle for rational concepts was made even more difficult by the

gradual realization he detested girls and adored men. He promptly responded by falling in love with youths who refused to acknowledge he existed. Every day he watched virile specimens jauntily parading up and down schoolhalls wearing skintight jeans and holding the hands of some bitch. It was too much!

On a different level, there was still relentless pressure to remain Pure For Jesus. (He had long since rationalized that his "failing" didn't count!) Given his attitudes towards women, this ought not have been hard; yet his daydreams about men gradually became more and more graphic. These ideas frightened him.

About the time Samuel turned seventeen, a group of breakaway fundamentalists founded a new church not far from the Mathis home. Samuel never attended church regularly because his parents had no car and were indifferent about church attendance. Neighbor ladies (those eternally "helpful" souls) often would offer him a ride, but it was a haphazard arrangement. The new church lay directly on the path to the river, and Samuel, an inveterate walker, always ambled down to the river of a Sunday. The Mathis' routine included a large noonday Sunday dinner, after which the father and mother would nap. Samuel, glad of an opportunity to escape their restrictive custody, would go walking. The river provided a suitable destination. It was on one such stroll that Samuel first saw Brother Amos.

Samuel had heard about Brother Amos but until now had never viewed the man. Brother Amos was the preacher of the breakaway congregation. He and his new church had attracted considerable attention in the small community.

The area Samuel inhabited was one of those small, rural farming societies where gossip was rampant and enjoyed with the gusto of modern-day beer drinkers fighting over particular brands of brew. Since the community was "dry," gossip went a long way towards providing a certain stimulation.

Brother Amos had turned up out of nowhere: that is to say, no one knew his parents, his ancestry, nor, in fact, anything about the man. As is the wont of certain fundamentalist sects, he was allowed to speak at a "meeting." A mistake from start to finish! Brother Amos had a voice as loud and resonant as any in the land. He was a man of extraordinary looks, possessing red, carroty hair, a strangely white-tanned skin and eyes which pierced one's soul. He was charismatic to the core. In less than six months he split up one church, siphoned off the membership of several others and had his own house of worship erected by grateful countryfolk.

Much of Brother Amos' success lay in his ability to make his followers feel guilty. He could make men ashamed of having relations with their *own* wives, much less those of other men. His parishioners were not smart people; they found it more enjoyable going about their sinful lives after being mightily chastized every Sunday. When Brother Amos roared denunciations at them, they felt small, cheap and disgusting—which made it easier during the following week to commit acts which might draw forth further condemnation. Those who sunk deepest into the muck of sin and degradation had the best chance of rising to sanctified sainthood. It was such a *comforting* notion.

Brother Amos appeared to be a great believer in the avoidance of temptation. In *his* church, men sat on one side of the aisle, women on the other. If now and then a couple of men seemed to be sitting rather close to one another, it was put down to crowded conditions. Among the types of followers Brother Amos attracted, some sins never registered. This was surprising, as he was eternally preaching against sins of the flesh. The parishioners loved it. They got to hear X-rated filth shouted at them at the top of Brother Amos' lungs—a ferocious sound indeed. True, such sins were *condemned*, as was right and proper, but it was so enjoyable *hearing* about them! Certain naive worshipers learned things they'd never known before. It was an exciting time!

As summer deepened, the new church held baptisms. In this most sacred of rituals, Brother Amos had his own way of doing things. For example, he again forced men and women into separate enclaves. If a Sister was to be joined to the Lord, he administered the rite quickly and perfunctorily. If a Brother were joining the Elect, the process usually took longer. In any case, parishioners seldom were allowed to view much. Brother Amos deemed it unseemly for the celebrant to be observed closely in wet, dripping robes. Some folks found their minister a bit of a kill-joy. In the past, half the fun of baptisms had been the opportunity to see bodies outlined underneath robes. Still, secure in the knowledge of their minister's State Of Grace, all willingly abided by his decision.

One brilliant Sunday afternoon, Samuel strolled down to the river, to his usual place, prepared to read a book he had lugged along. The day was so hot, however, and the water moved so languidly, that he soon fell asleep. He was awakened, sometime thereafter, by a slight sound. As he glanced round, he saw Brother Amos, naked, changing clothes after having performed a baptism.

Samuel knew he ought not watch, but he could no more have stopped himself than he could have spoken. The scene was one of indescribable beauty to the young man. Brother Amos rubbed himself vigorously with a towel he'd brought along, and, unaware he was being observed, the preacher allowed the sun to warm his chilled body. Brother Amos was a splendid man. He was the first *grown* man Samuel had ever seen nude; and the youth was amazed by his anatomy. Amazed, aroused—and in love! He prayed the man would dress and leave without knowing a spectator was lurking about. And, in time, that was what happened.

The episode had a profound impact on Samuel. Not long after his view of Brother Amos by the river, he began attending the breakaway church.

Brother Amos' tabernacle was of a type which must be attended to be believed. Even observing the congregation in action, a nonbeliever could easily come away without a true understanding of what had transpired before his eyes.

The intensity in the little church was palpable. There was never an intellectual basis for the congregation's belief—their grasp of God was always emotional. Primitive people, denying themselves everything except the joy of worship—when they entered the house of their Lord, all inhibitions were unleashed. Brother Amos was an expert at eliciting raw passions from his parishioners, in a subtle, yet powerful fashion.

Samuel, as he aged, tried approaching God on a more mature level. Inwardly, he was appalled by what he saw, but Brother Amos so captivated him, he could not stay away from the country temple. On more than one occasion it seemed to him the eyes of the preacher were on *him*, boring into his soul, reading all the lust which was etched there. The strangest thing about the feeling was that no shame accompanied it. Samuel grew confused, and after a time, his confusion was noticed.

It came about on a Sunday when the congregation's antics were especially outrageous.

Brother Amos was always an integrated part of the whole mass of worshipers. The situation was analogous to a conductor of a symphonic orchestra. Brother Amos led off with his sermon, slow and sonorous at first, before building to crescendic bellows which in turn were echoed and hurled back at him by his followers. As the rhythm of the people rose, moved and shifted, strange and unsettling things were liable to occur. The men's section would emit groans, shouts, moans; the female's side would respond with shrieks, cries and dances. By the end of a service, Brother Amos often would be hoarse; his followers exhausted. On the Sunday in question, Samuel was in his accustomed place at the rear of the church. (Despite his desire to be as close as possible to his strange lover, he was afraid to move nearer the pulpit.) The tempo of the meeting was in flux, moving from fast to torrid. A large, robust lady, in a fit of divine ecstasy, burst out of the women's section like a cow loosed out of a truck and began a dance of exaltation, urged on by both Brother Amos and the congregation.

As dancing was "sinful," the woman dared not exhibit formal training had she possessed any. Her dance consisted of hops and jerks, much like a rabbit investigating a spring garden in speeded-up motion. She was large-bosomed and each jump threatened to destroy the integrity of her garments. She was a sight. Brother Amos began "preaching" faster; the lady bounced about in keeping with his words, until without warning she uttered a dreadful howl, rolled her large, bovinelike eyes heavenward, danced faster and began "speaking in tongues." It was

an eerie sound, half shout, half song: an a capella disco, long before the days of Donna Summer. Her breasts bounced vigorously
with each gyration and turned her into an unleashed gargoyle.
In this frenzy of "divine" inspiration she soon was joined by
others, both men and women, all clomping about in their Sunday
best. This hellish vision continued at some length, to be brought
to a shattering climax by an extended roar of "Hallelujah!" from
Brother Amos.

The congregation collapsed in sweaty exhaustion.

Slowly, everyone began filing out. No words were spoken
after the last shout by Brother Amos.

Samuel, in tears, stumbled from the church. He was moved to
weep for the splendid man he loved, dismayed by the grossness
of what he had witnessed. Caught up in his inner turmoil, he did
not see Brother Amos move up behind him. A strong hand
clasped him on the shoulder and spun him around.

He found himself looking into the hypnotic eyes of his lover/
priest.

"You are in need of private prayer, Brother. Come with me!"

Dumbly Samuel followed Brother Amos to the small house behind the church where he lived. There he led Samuel into a
small, stark chamber. Striding to the middle of the room, Brother
Amos grasped Samuel's hands.

"Kneel with me!" he commanded.

Samuel obeyed, conscious not of God, or whatever words
Brother Amos was uttering but only of the man himself. The minister's rough, strong hands were still holding his own—caress-
ing them. The scent of sweat which permeated Brother Amos
from his recent exertions in the pulpit was strong. The nearness
of his idol drove all thoughts of God and Jesus from Samuel's
mind. In that instant, Samuel saw clearly why religion de-
nounced sex. He understood why his love for the man far out-
shone all love he had ever felt for "God." In one blinding, stag-
gering moment of truth, Samuel realized that the "God" thrust
upon gullible mankind by Christians could not exist. Like a
Christian undergoing the subjective emotional tidal wave of
"conversion," so in like fashion was Samuel swept from the de-

structive path of superstitious nonsense. He was not mature enough to venture beyond his one, enormous blasphemy. But of his verdict he was certain! By recognizing the true nature of *love*, Samuel intuitively comprehended the Christian's great lie: "God is love." If *one* facet of the faith was a lie, the whole structure fell in shambles of disarray. Samuel's new "God" was the man beside him; "God" was himself, his existence and the love he felt for Brother Amos. "Hell" was knowing he dared not profess his love. He shuddered at the desecration of being forced to silence. Brother Amos, feeling the youth trembling beside him, clasped Samuel's shoulders, looked deep into the boy's soul and said, surprisingly gently, "I shall baptize thee into the faith! You are ready!"

Samuel, struggling to assert his new-found freedom, was commanded to silence by Brother Amos.

"Say nothing. I *know* your mind! God knows your mind! Surrender your soul to the *force* which fills you!"

Denial was on the tip of Samuel's tongue, but he could not shove the words beyond his lips. So close to Brother Amos, so near the man's warm flesh and daring, parted lips, he had no will of his own. He bowed his head in submission. Not to "God," but to love.

Brother Amos cupped his hand beneath Samuel's chin and raised his head. Their eyes met. "I *know* your mind," the preacher repeated. "I know your heart. I understand your soul! Trust *me*, as you would God."

The plans for Samuel's baptism moved forward. They included several meetings with Brother Amos and a group of young men he called his Disciples of the Way. The gatherings were conducted in an atmosphere of great spirituality, but for all that, Samuel found himself wondering if he wasn't slowly losing his mind. He *seemed* so much at home with the group—yet he sensed his attachment to God, Jesus and religion was irretrievably shattered. He loved Brother Amos but saw no possibility of realizing his love. It was similar to loving God, in that loving God had always been an emotion which mingled fear with hopelessness. Fear of dying without "Jesus" and helplessness because

"God's" conditions were impossible for a *human being* to achieve. Samuel did not want to love Brother Amos in such a fashion.

Samuel, however, was not brave. Baptism day dawned. He could find no way out of the ordeal and finally decided to go through with the ritual. It wouldn't make any *difference*. It wouldn't *change* anything—and it *would* bring him closer to Brother Amos. One more chance to feel those hands . . .

There was a considerable crowd on the river bank when Samuel arrived. Two women were being baptized before him and these rites were casually carried out. Samuel was given a robe and led to a sheltered area by two strong, well-muscled Disciples of the Way. They watched appreciatively as Samuel disrobed. He was embarrassed by their interest even while knowing he should not be. Habits long ingrained were hard to break. They led him past the watchers on the bank, who eyed him with disinterest—he had never succeeded in becoming one of them. People began wandering off.

The day was hot, the water warm. The Disciples led Samuel into midriver where Brother Amos waited. Samuel hesitated briefly. Even for love he disliked misleading the preacher. The Disciples, however, had each grabbed an arm and were now half-dragging him into the middle of the stream. The water was over waist deep.

At last he stood before Brother Amos.

The crowd on the bank was far away. Brother Amos looked hard into Samuel's eyes and spoke.

"Are you ready to offer yourself to *your* God?"

Samuel could not force himself to say "yes," so he stood mute, realizing suddenly that Brother Amos' hand was beneath the water, beneath the baptismal robe, groping his crotch. At the very peak of his young virility, Samuel could not stop his organ from responding. To his utter amazement he sensed Brother Amos was manipulating him to a sexual climax—in full view of the staid congregation! As Brother Amos achieved his goal, Samuel felt the hands of the Disciples close over his nose and mouth and he was immersed into the water.

## Baptism

Rising, shaking river water from his face, Samuel heard the low, powerful voice of his lover/priest.

"I have baptized thee in the name of Eros. You are one of us, Samuel; men who love one another in the *true* sense of love. In ancient times Christians hid themselves amongst the Roman populace; now I place myself amongst them! My ministry is dedicated to rescuing souls like yours, joining you together with like spirits, that you may comfort one another, never again suffering the loneliness of outcasts or the mockery of those fools on the bank who watch us and see not! Arise my son, my brother! Go forth without fear! I have baptized thee into a new freedom, whose faith arises within thyself!"

# Where Have All The Heroes Gone?

Every time I pick up a new book or short story with a homosexual theme, I get excited. Maybe *this* will be the one! Maybe at last I'm going to embark on an adventure with an honest-to-goodness HERO! I start reading. By the time I've reached the end of the first chapter, first page, or, sometimes, the first damned paragraph, it's apparent that I'm in for a letdown.

Invariably, the protagonist turns out to be some nut who's so spaced out on dope, booze or feelings of inadequacy, no self-respecting man would want to know the bastard, much less have a relationship with him—even in a fantasy.

Where have all the heroes gone? Why don't authors give us men worthy of admiration? I'm tired, tired, tired of reading (or hearing about) losers! Give me a winner for a change! I want a hero! I want a guy on a white horse (well, a white Corvette will do in a pinch) to come charging down the hillside, throw me over his shoulder and carry me off into that beautiful sunset! And I don't want the jerk so wiped out of his mind he can't tell me from the horse!

I've almost given up reading, I'm so depressed about the state of "gay" fiction. There certainly isn't anything gay about the leading men being pushed down our throats these days.

But perhaps the writers aren't entirely to blame. Most of the places in which we pick up guys don't lend themselves to the hero concept. Dim, dingy bars so full of noise and smoke you can't see what you're getting in the first place, and couldn't

*Where Have All The Heroes Gone?*

hear the trick of the hour spout an idea if his head were clear
enough to contain one. Sure, I went through that routine — we
all do at one time or another — usually when we first hit the
"streets." We're liberated, we tell ourselves, unsure what it is
we've left behind  and scared as hell about the things we're
going to find ahead of us. The only solution seems to be popping
pills, swilling booze and whispering archly-aimed trash about
one another into the ears of all who'll listen. Who the hell are we
fooling?

I've given up all that. The bars, the baths, the dope and the
booze. I decided, at the over-the-hill age of thirty-six, that I know
what I want! Such arrogance is surely doomed to failure from
the beginning. Filled with  zero expectations, however, I can
aim for the sky. Bombs bursting in air and that trembly sensation
in the pit of your stomach just before the first kiss. I'm gonna
have it all or nothing. I'm gonna find me a hero.

Now don't ask me to *define* my dream man. You can't pin
heroes down like butterflies under glass. None of this "he's got
to be six-feet-three, look like a matinee idol and hung like Cae-
sar's horse" crap for me. Heroes are like gods — you know 'em
when you find 'em. The thing is, be prepared. Like a princess in
a fairy tale, you've got to be READY. In *those* stories, princes
pop up all over the place: in nutshells, out of frogskins, leaping
over walls — you name it, a prince either turned into it or emerged
out of it. *You just have to be ready!* Tomorrow is too late to become the perfect you.

Being ready means different things to different people; it de-
pends on your definition of a hero. If you're looking for an
award-winning bodybuilder, you'd damn well better be prepared
to work your *own* ass off (especially if you're a blubber-butt). If
your idea of god on earth is Susie Siren the drag queen, I guess
you simply keep your wigs dry. Even with my head in the clouds,
I'm not *completely* unrealistic. Knowing what I wanted, I worked
like hell, getting myself in shape to meet my hero.

I followed a rigorous exercise schedule, kept the house picked
up and the cat's litter box cleaned. Gradually my flesh responded
to the unnatural demands I made of it. My progress, however,

was not without side effects.

As my body grew solid and strong, my expectations rose to match my achievements. Having given up drugs, booze and, yes, even those damned poppers, all my friends felt I'd lost my marbles and began avoiding me. I can't say I minded this, because once my head cleared and I began to *think* for the first time in a couple of years, the foolishness of using such mind-altering substances readily became apparent. Instead of escaping *into* a world of my own making, I was using all that stuff as a crutch. I didn't need those things anymore—my friends did. They resented me and I grew disgusted with them. Sad, in a way, but feeling healthy, fit and *free* for the first time in many a long, dark night, I was no longer willing to go back down their road. I was heading for the sunshine—and a hero.

There were other difficulties. The worst, no doubt, became my arrogance. As I continued "gettingready" ("gettingready" is a neverceasing activity), I grew arrogant. When you used to be a fat, not very attractive two-hundred-pounder and you turn into a man strong, powerful and masculine enough to turn heads, it does something to you. All right. I admit it, I'm arrogant! I worked hard getting where I am—you'd be keen on yourself too! When that "duckling" became a swan, it didn't fly south with the ducks, did he? Hell, no!

So. At last you're ready. Ready. And alone. Losers need each other to keep up their courage. It takes a lot of guts to refuse to throw away crutches and fly. Banding together, the losers of the world are ever-ready with excuses for their delays. They'll get off pills—tomorrow. They'll lose forty pounds—next month. Years go by and before long, they're looking backward saying, "It's too late." Bullshit! It's *never* too late. Just as with self-abasement, there's no time limit on self-improvement.

Having reached a peak of perfection, you're ready for the search.

Heroes can turn up anywhere at anytime. But there is something about the human animal which makes us all impatient. We hate to wait. So, cautiously, hesitantly (where the hell do you go looking for heroes?) you start going out. Walking the streets, visiting whatever places you've decided your special brand of hero might frequent.

That's where I ran into trouble.

Like I said, the process of "gettingready" changes you. It changed me. I like the changes, love 'em even. Feeling good, I look better. Knowing what I'd accomplished with simple strength of will made me (I admit it) impatient with those who have no will and no strength. The solitude, which at first translates as loneliness, gradually becomes aloneness—which is an entire world of difference. I got to the point I enjoyed being by myself, I loved waking up with the whole day before me, twenty-four hours when HE might show up, no time to lay abed, on with the show. I dressed, snapped my small, attractive lambda pin on my collar and hit the street.

I live in a city of about a quarter-million; large enough for at least one good-sized hero, you'd think. This particular morning I had a destination in mind, so I wasn't overtly on the prowl for the man of my dreams. (It's best not to really *look* for heroes— like with fairy princesses, let *them* find *you*!) The day was beautiful, I was in fine spirits and looked, I suppose, more arrogant than usual. My mind, as was its wont, was occupied with a world of its own. All male. Turning a corner, I ran (almost literally) into a raucous parade.

A street preacher had set up operations.

He was an itinerate type, one of those who shout at the top of their raspy voices, in an old-fashioned singsongy tone which would grate on the nerves of angels in heaven, if there were angels or heavens and assuming such beings were possessed of nerves.

This guy looked worse than most of those who resort to sidewalk proselytizing. He was dressed in shabby trousers and a faded flannel shirt which was topped with a worn suit-coat, open at the neck. He was holding a Bible (at least I assume it was a Bible—could have been a catalogue of porno for all I know) aloft in one hand. His other appendage was being flung about in wild abandon. From time to time he hopped up and down on his feet like a large bluejay searching for worms.

He was a sight!

A crowd had gathered to listen to him. Anytime a fool such as this gets up and starts ranting there are always other idiots willing to stop and listen. Faded women, dull and wornout from life. Men who have failed and are fearful the sputtering words of such sidewalk Jesuses are truths. These all listened with rapt attention as the walking specter from Gehenna catalogued their deplorable condition. If a man were filled with real human compassion, such sights would be partitioned from reality, set up as sideshows in the arena of despair.

Having emerged from my personal hell by dint of my own efforts, I have little sympathy with the cellars other people inhabit. Our punishments, more often than not, are of our own choosing. Fate and circumstances seldom condemn anyone to disaster. Our failures, too, stem from volitional acts, compounded only by weakness and stupidity.

I was in no mood to waste time with such a nut this morning. My arrogance was showing something fierce. Rounding the corner, I almost bumped into the old man.

He turned on me, his wild eyes red and bloodshot (I always wonder about that—don't these people ever sleep?), and began dancing and shouting.

"Repent sinner! God has led you here today. Accept the message of the Lord! REPENT!"

Having nothing to repent of except my lateness at discovering all the latent goodness in myself, life and the quest for heroes, I tried sidestepping his scrawny hand. I said nothing, but my eyes must have poured forth my contempt for the fellow and his "philosophy." Taking my silence for tacit fear, he fell into step beside me, while his followers formed a Pied Piper's band behind us.

"Accept the Lord Jesus, young man!" he screamed at me.

I tried being funny.

"He's not my type—too skinny."

The preacher didn't like frivolity. In fact, he was a right irritable old cuss. Has to be to do all that kneeling and praying. Such an *unnatural* position—must give 'em stomach cramps. He reached out and grabbed my arm, while reverting back to his initial moldy messages, "Repent, sinner! The end is near. The Rapture of the Lord will soon be upon us! Get ready! Accept Christ and be prepared!"

Well! I ask you? I'd been getting ready for years by this time. He had some nerve!

"I'm as prepared as I'm going to be, old man," I hissed at him. (Why not? He was certainly villainous!) "Just bugger off and leave me be!"

"It's my *duty* to preach the Word Of God," he bellowed in my ear. (WHY do they assume everyone is deaf?) "Those who hear but hear not are doomed—" He broke off, his bloodshot eyes grew wide with horror. He'd spied my lambda pin. His hand, unfortunately, gripped me tighter.

"Sinner! You dare wear the sign of Sodom and Gomorrah? Repent, you son of Satan! God can forgive even you!"

"How kind," I grunted. "And you're quite wrong—it's only a sign of Sodomy; we're not interested in Gomo. You'd do well to turn loose my sleeve."

"Sinner, SINNER!" (Ouch!) "Why persist in your foolish folly? Repent today! I will pray with you—the blood of Jesus will save you! Think about it! The Blessed Saving Grace of Je-sus! How can you refuse HIM?"

All this was delivered in his singsongy voice. He did have a rhythm about him, and by the time we reached this stage of the incident, several of those who were following behind us began singing and chanting "Je-sus saves! Je-sus saves!" in a sort of strange unison with the old man. I was getting decidedly annoyed with the whole pack of them. I've always hated such people, not to mention the "ideas" they supposedly represent. You know how it is—once in a while something makes you so mad, you'd just love to haul off and smack somebody—anybody—who keeps spouting foolishness. Most of the time there's no honorable way you can deliver yourself of such frustrations. You can't, rationally, go around socking everyone on the nose just because you don't agree with their whacky notions. At the same time, these Christians have been a bane upon us for centuries. I've long wanted to punch out a few of 'em.

"Just let go, old man," I told him again. "There's nothing I'd love more than knocking the hell out of you. Turn loose!"

"Je-sus! Enter the heart of this Stubborn Sinner!" was his response. I daresay by now he was so stoned on his own words, he didn't realize what was going on. We had walked possibly half the block by this time. His adherents had so crowded around us that movement was becoming difficult. I'd had enough. I reached back and let him have a punch right in the kisser. Boy, did it feel good! Unfurtunately, it didn't jar loose the old goat's viselike grip on my shirt. Neither did it endear me to the rest of the parade. In fact, they became downright nasty. I've got to confess I hadn't expected the whole bunch to jump me (whatever happened to that turning of the cheek business?), but that's what happened. In a few seconds, a general melee was underway. I was greatly outnumbered and having a difficult time keeping my feet, when suddenly there's this blond guy beside me, swinging away at these turkeys.

I muttered a word of thanks between swings but he seemed to be enjoying himself. Before long, sirens announced the arrival of the cops. The fight was quickly broken up and we were all led off to the police station. What a day *this* was turning out to be!

It was to get worse.

The "minister" decided I was an agent of the devil and swore out a warrant for *my* arrest, charging *I* had attacked *him*! The cops, sympathetic at first, were less so when they spotted my lambda pin. Still, the facts of the matter were clearly beyond even *their* ability to distort, and they had already committed themselves to the *facts* before they noticed the pin!

The blond guy who'd pitched in to help had disappeared.

To top the day's achievement was the fact the affair would have to be settled in court. The "preacher" insisted! Lucky me—I got released on my own recognizance.

I'd had it! Over the next few weeks I put aside my search for a hero and concentrated on my legal problelms. The fact I was a homosexual became well-publicized. I wanted it that way. I am tired of the bullshit we have to put up with. *Somebody* has to take a stand, and my case was wonderfully made for *good* publicity! I simply couldn't pass up the opportunity to score some points for the "cause."

Well, there isn't any sense in going into details about the court case. It was *not* a Perry Mason cliffhanger. As soon as it *reached* court, a judge threw the whole thing out, awarded me court costs and fined the preacher for contempt when the old bastard started raving about "ungodliness" on the bench. The press had a field day and for once homos weren't pictured as the villains. I ate it up.

Finally, however, the last interview was given and the last flashbulb popped. I left the court building and was walking down the block to where I'd parked my bicycle when I spotted someone who looked familiar. Looked good, too!

We gazed at each other across the expanse of street.

It dawned on me it was the guy who'd pitched in when I was fighting that mob of fanatics.

I'd never gotten time to thank him. From his absence, however, it was plain he had not wanted to get involved. With all the press coverage labeling me a queer, he was, no doubt, less interested than usual in being drawn into a sensational affair. But I wanted to go up and thank him. After all, I owed him that. While I was standing awkwardly on the street making up my mind, he moved suddenly in my direction.

We met before we exchanged any words. He appeared very diffident but finally spoke. "I guess you're pissed, aren't you?"

Actually I hadn't thought about being angry: self-preservation is too strong a virtue. We all do what we must. He'd jumped in when I needed help. If he was hesitant about getting caught up in the rest of it, who could blame him? Not me.

We conversed a couple of minutes, superficial items. It seemed plain there was something weighing on the guy's mind. I didn't know how to put him at ease, casualness having never been my forte. Besides, the longer I looked at him, the better I liked him—and the more I wanted him. My hero? Well, he *had* rescued me—sort of. It would sure as hell do for a start.

He had the goodlooks of a boy-next-door type, handsome,

rugged without having had to put in all the work I'd done. Such effortless muscularity always makes me jealous. His face was close to being perfect, except for the fact his eyes kept darting about, fearful of being caught and held by my own.

Standing on the streetcorner wasn't my idea of the perfect mating place. I suggested a nearby beer parlor. He accepted, which surprised me. I expected him to have an "engagement" elsewhere. The place, fortunately, was near-empty. The bartender, who recognized me both from my infrequent visits to the place as well as my recent notoriety, was effusive in his praise of what I'd done. The praise was nice, but overdone. I'd simply been in the right place at the wrong time, or vice versa, depending on your viewpoint. We sat down at a corner table, out of the way of general traffic.

He took a drink of beer, stared into his glass and mumbled. "I was afraid of getting involved."

So what else is new? I wouldn't have gotten involved either, if the sons-of-bitches hadn't jumped me! "Nothing wrong with that," I told him. "Hell, you saved me from getting banged up by that crowd of creeps. Most people wouldn't have done that much."

"I heard him mention your lambda pin," the guy replied.

I sat still as a mouse. Now it was *my* turn to become diffident. Of all the turns the conversation might have taken, this would have been the last I'd have predicted.

"I figured *that* was what kept you away," I said without thinking.

"It was," he said, his face flushing red under his late summer tan. "I . . . I'm not really . . . comfortable with the idea." He shut up for a second, then rushed on as if he had to spit out his thoughts before they choked him.

"Before, it was always something to be ashamed of. Meeting people in dark holes, furtive affairs, never finding anyone you'd want to introduce to friends . . . I never . . . met a hero before." Having said that much, he lapsed into a very confused silence which grew because I was too shocked to give a sensible reply.

ME? A HERO?

You gotta be kidding!

He wasn't though . . .

I could tell, the guy *really* admired me. The idea that *I* —that an ordinary man could do anything heroic, never crossed my mind. I'd been so busy looking for my own special dream I'd sort of let reality slip away. In this stygian century, *all* homosexual men and women are heroes and heroines, simply by virtue of living from day to day. We catch so much hell from those "normal" bastards around us that when we manage to keep our lives together, from one hour to the next, without losing our reason, we've done something important. Some of us don't make it, true. *Those* are the ones you see spaced out all the time on some damned mind-altering substance. But for everyone who succumbs to such easy temptation, there are hundreds like the guy sitting across from me, uncertain, unsure, but headed in the right direction.

"I'm sorry," he mumbled, breaking into my chain of emotions. "I better go." He started to rise.

"Why?" I asked, staring at him. "As far as I'm concerned, you're the hero in this affair. I'd like to get to know you better. In every sense of the word." I grinned impishly. "Platonically, physically—even 'Biblically.' "

I sighed with relief as he slowly sat back down. God, he was beautiful! Heroes don't crop up every day. I sure didn't want to lose this one a second time!

# A Passionate Attachment

"The depths of sin in which this sorry world mires itself never cease to amaze me!" The minister spoke the words to his audience with a certain measure of enthusiasm.

"I have here," he continued, holding aloft a bluish bit of paper, "a *deplorable* tract from a man who dares call himself a *Christian Minister*! A practicing, nonrepentant Sodomite — who in the name of Je-sus lures young men and boys into a web of sin and degradation!" Appalled murmurs lifted from the congregation. "How wrathful our Lord must feel at the use of . . ." The minister was off and running, his booming voice thundering out over his flock like a foghorn, piercing their passive ignorance. Angrily, he crumpled the bluish bit of paper. It lay atop the pulpit for a time, until an exceptional thump by the pastor sent the offending document bouncing onto the floor. It rolled beneath the lectern and there it remained, unnoticed, except by one alert pair of eyes . . .

James Walker saw the paper. From the startling moment the preacher uttered the word Sodomite, James knew he *had* to get his hands on that tract! James, seventeen, recently had admitted to himself that he was attracted to men. Knowing such desires were sinful, he dutifully prayed long and hard over the matter. Seeing that bit of blue winking at him from beneath the pulpit, James knew God had heard and answered those prayers.

Obtaining the paper proved simple: James hung around after

the service and offered to help with the cleaning-up. His father, a ranking deacon, always insisted on grabbing "a few words" with "the Reverend." These "few words" often seemed a sermon in themselves.

Riding home with the family, James was in a sweat, fearful someone would hear the incriminating document in his pocket. Every time he shifted position it crackled like thunder . . .

Hours passed before the youth, trembling, smoothed out his treasure. He read it entranced—feeling great warmth fill his soul.

The tract proclaimed itself a product of the Confederated Ministries of Jesus and explained briefly several projects sponsored by the organization. Typed on the back of the tract was a personal message from the preacher who operated the Ministries: ". . . I am 5'10", 215 pounds . . . despite the fact I was born in 1931, *everyone* says I look *much* younger than my years! I am a devout *Christian Minister*, dedicted to helping fellow Gays learn the truth about God and Jesus. I am looking for a life-mate . . . my interests revolve around the ?-22 age group . . ." The message ran on for several more paragraphs. James, for all his innocence, understood the gist of it. He hoped he'd be the sort of guy the minister—a man with the fanciful name of Donegal Mac-Clintock (call me Mac!)—would take a liking to. A fat, old man with youthful notions was not exactly what James dreamed about in the quiet stillness of his room at night, but a Good Christian Man would no doubt be hard to find in a city like Atlanta. A man's character was more important to James than . . . all that other stuff. Knowing "Mac," James felt, would give him an advantage.

James packed his few things one Tuesday night, wrapped his battered satchel in a plastic "dime-store" raincoat and hid the bundle along the road he'd take the next evening. Wednesday, and a desire to attend prayer meetin', provided James with his opportunity. He picked up his gear, changed from church clothes into jeans and a sturdy shirt and headed for town, two miles away. Once there, he phoned his mother, saying he'd like to stay overnight with a friend, "If'n it was all right?" The sad, tired woman agreed, unaware she was speaking to her son for the last time. Exhilarated, and a little frightened, James rushed towards the dark serpent of super highway which pointed northward to Atlanta.

He arrived safely, a fact astonishing to anyone much over seventeen, but James, in his naivete and youth, believed himself indestructible. There were still people oblivious to the danger-quotient involving hitchhikers. Sixteen hours after he'd left his small, secure community, James was dumped off on a bit of roadway directly beneath the towering Atlanta skyline. He'd never been to the city before—Valdosta was the largest place he'd ever seen, and it didn't compare. Tired now, unsure about his initial wisdom in setting out, he trudged the miles needed to reach downtown Atlanta. From there, he sought and received directions to Texas Avenue and the headquarters of Mac's "Confederated Ministries."

Donegal MacClintock was an energetic man. A "live-wire!" Given everything he set himself to accomplish, he had to be. His friends continuously expressed amazement at his energy. He assured them God looked after His own—the work of the Ministries was far too important to be entrusted to a man of lackadaisical temperament! The fact Mac constantly prowled the city in search of youngmen was only one aspect of his exuberant nature. He would have felt guilty if God's work were not finished before embarking on his own projects. Not that he any longer bothered separating the two.

Mac was perpetually annoyed at the gay community's reaction towards God and religion. True, significant numbers of his gay brothers professed belief, but few toiled in the vineyard. And lately, more and more appeared to be scoffers, disbelievers, even . . . atheists! How could anyone not believe? How dare anyone not believe! Mac's cheerful face darkened dangerously at the notion of disbelief.

As the new wave of fundamentalist fervor rose and broke across the land, condemning homosexuality, howling for the heads of "Christian" adherents who retained a foot in both camps, Mac found himself in demand—needed to explain to wavering homosexuals why their current condemnation was part of God's Great Design. This new persecution stemmed from their sinful natures—but not, he always pointed out, the "sin" of homosexuality. Being gay wasn't a sin; the only sin was involvement in casual, unloving sex with multitudes of strangers. Gays, Mac reasoned, were suffering now much like the Children of Israel had suffered in Egypt. Paying for past misdeeds. In the future, in that rosy afterlife, all would be changed! God created gay people, too, Mac eagerly exclaimed to all who'd listen. The prospect of a new convert cheered Mac immensely. There were never enough hours in his days as he bounced here and there, seeking lost souls to rescue.

Mac's gaiety, the pleasure he found in his busy life, made him a magnet for a great variety of men. Some came to Mac because they had nowhere else to turn, others were drawn to him because God and Mac's Christian Ministries offered them what they perceived to be a Higher Purpose. These were usually older men, lonely, ever in doubt that God really loved *Them*! Sucking cocks was all very well on a late Saturday night, when they'd drunk themselves bleary-eyed; but it became disgusting when confronted in the light of sunny Sunday mornings and they heard God's call to prayer and repentance. Hangovers and guilt were Mac's faithful assistants.

No such doubts troubled Mac! Long, long ago, he'd made up his mind he could enjoy both God and men. Having reached this comforting decision, he set about justifying it to himself. He succeeded so well he was able to cease considering the situation in terms of a "problem." On the few occasions he condescended to debate antigay clerics, his bright, aggressive presentations usually carried the day.

James' appearance happily coincided with the arrival at Mac's Ministries of a bountiful check from a grateful "benefactor." The check's presence placed Mac in a particularly joyous frame of mind.

The unexpected largess sent Mac racing to his piano where

he was banging out an upbeat version of "Swing Low, Sweet Chariot" when James tentatively rang the bell of the rundown house. Striding towards the door, Mac warbled his own version of the lyrics: "I looked over Jor-dan and what did I see? A band of youngmen coming after me . . ." Throwing open the door he saw the idealized vision of his youngman standing hesitantly in front of him.

"Hello!" Mac exclaimed, smiling widely. "What may I do for You?"

"I found his here note . . ." James began, offering the paper awkwardly to the fat man at the door. The farmboy's courage almost failed him in the face of Mac's startling presence.

The flamboyant minister was attired in a pale orange shirt, the color of the sun having an offday in the beaming department. This was topped by a bright, lime-green suit of polyester. Since Mac filled all corners of the suit, the completed image was that of a gelatin mousse spilled onto a floor of orange linoleum.

Taking the worn bit of blue paper, Mac excitedly ushered his unexpected guest indoors. James was offered milk and some food. Grace was pronounced over the meal, allaying the farmboy's fears that Mac might not be a good, God-fearing man. The minister was not without talents and soon extracted the story of James' troubled attempts at reconciling God with the urge for sex with men. Mac was forever grateful that during this difficult period neither the phone nor doorbell interrupted the delicate climate needed to assure James his decision in traveling to Mac's sanctuary was a wise one.

At the end of their conversation, Mac generously offered James a bed in the ramshackle old house. The fact that after a couple of days Mac went with the bed (he was never one to rush things) seemed only fair to James. They soon settled themselves into a domestic arrangement which was very pleasing to Mac.

James, having no experience by which to judge the situation, accepted it as God's plan. Mac was obviously a good man. Prayers were uttered regularly and with great seriousness. Mac was busy every day helping men come to terms with themselves and their place in God's Scheme of Things. He helped suicidal souls return to the fold, more secure in God's Great Love, less anxious when their trick of the night before grew critical and abusive by light of day.

Sex with Mac didn't seem so bad either. Any uneasiness James experienced, he attributed to himself, rather than to Mac or the situation.

Mac, after all, was consumed by the Holy Spirit.

Mac's friends and parishioners were a different matter.

These, for the most part, consisted of aged queens who flitted about, swishing their overly fat, or excruciatingly thin, asses this way or that, all the while gazing longingly into James' eyes. Oftentimes the hands of these folk suddenly appeared on private parts of James' body. The young man found this embarrassing but seldom said or did anything. At first he mentioned the matter to Mac, but Mac's only reaction was to giggle and mumble something about girls being girls. James didn't follow the remark, since, in his first two weeks in Atlanta, he'd not seen a woman anywhere near Mac, although there had been a couple whom he'd thought were women, but weren't. It was very confusing.

Besides these older men, there were much younger males, thin as rails, arty, whatever that was. James assumed at first it was a disease accounting for the thinness since all possessed it. Sunday mornings, when Mac officiated at the major worship service of the week, James found himself thinking that if the older men exchanged a few pounds with the younger group, everyone would be better off. They looked a sight! A fleeting grin flickered across his face. The brief smile made him so angelical, several older dears almost fainted, only retaining their grips on consciousness by plotting ways they might successfully pry the golden youth away from Mac.

After some weeks, James, who had been seeking work, found employment as a mechanic at a garage on Myland Avenue, a site not far from Mac's Ministries. James was good with motors and mechanical things and this aptitude, coupled wi th his conscientiousness, made him a valuable addition to the garage's workforce.

James, taciturn from shyness, found himself taking his lunch break with another mechanic scarcely older than himself. They talked of one thing and another, gradually forming a tenuous type of comradeship. Consuming their meal one sunny afternoon, James' attention turned to a bar half a block down the street. His companion, Nate, noticed the interest.

"You lookin' at the Spur?" he queried.

"Not especially," James answered. "I don't drink. I ain't never been in a bar."

"The Spur's a queer-bar. Homo-sexuals." Nate said, clarifying his description. "You like girls—or guys?"

James, discomfited, made no reply.

Nate noticed the uneasiness and grinned. "Hell, man it ain't nothin' to worry about. *I* don't care. Nobody 'round here does. Jake—" he pointed to their fellow worker, pumping gas into a rich-looking El Dorado "—he's queer. Gay. Ask him to take you there some night if'n you wanna go. He says the Spur's the hottest bar in town."

Again James said nothing but his mind absorbed the news and filed it away. He looked at Jake with new interest. Jake was handsome. Far more in tune with James' youthful visions of male love than what he'd come to accept with Mac. The notion that Jake liked guys was intriguing but James felt a surge of guilt, of disloyalty over the thoughts he was entertaining. Resolutely, he put them out of his mind.

In spite of working at the station, James continued assisting Mac's ministries. As weeks passed, James became adept at handling the routine jobs connected with the institute's day-to-day operations. Other youngmen turned up with their tracts and were offered lodging in Mac's house. Sometimes James felt like he was in a hotel. Life in the city was enormously different from what the farmboy was accustomed to. He never would have believed there could be so many gay people in the whole world as he observed in Atlanta. That anyone would deny the existence of God was also beyond James' limited imagination—yet Mac assured him such was the case.

Mac, when all was said and done, considered James a godsend.

The youth had a native intelligence which could both retain and carry out Mac's instructions. The young man's presence so excited the old queens who called on the ministry for help that the income of the organization trebled during James' initial six months in residence. Being able to leave James at the ministry's headquarters allowed Mac more time to run around. He was often "too tired" to bother James at night, a situation the younger man soon found only mildly annoying.

At the service station, Jake finally got around to speaking to the shy, new kid. Nate and the others, deciding James must be gay, watched the initial rituals with interest.

James had tried (without much success) to refrain from thinking about Jake. James knew in his heart he was lusting after the man and considered this a sin against Jesus and an affront to Mac. Mac couldn't *help* his age or the fact he was heavier and less attractive than one might like. James believed he and Mac were a pair, drawn together to comfort one another and do God's work. He sensed, intuitively, that Jake, or someone like him, could easily become the serpent in this otherwise serene garden.

As page after page of the calendar disappeared, James, who had turned eighteen shortly after reaching Atlanta, found himself thinking about his forthcoming nineteenth birthday. At nineteen he could legally drink. Another temptation would come his way. He would be able to go into a bar if he wanted. It was sinful, but so much went on there . . .

The thought would not go away. James gradually found himself dissatisfied with his lot. Such unhappiness could only be the Devil tempting him, yet no amount of praying did any good. Mac wasn't much help, either. As James took over more and more work, and brought in more and more money, Mac began disappearing—sometimes for days. James tried, without much luck, to find out where the older man went. Whenever James questioned Mac about his absences, the minister simply smiled broadly and replied that all the wayward souls of the city did not come *seeking* Christ—like lost sheep, they had to be found.

For, to Mac's chagrin, he discovered his parishioners preferred James to himself. And it wasn't simply that James was young and attractive, though that *was* a part of it. James' sincerity was *so* apparent, his faith *so* real, he exposed Mac's venal nature. Mac *believed* eagerly enough, but his belief was jaded, old and worn out. Mac, of necessity, used the ministry as a livelihood. James used it to save souls. Mac had long since rationalized sexuality with spirituality, roped the pair together and bounded on through life. In James, these two forces were struggling, neither victorious, neither vanquished. As the battle raged, James, inwardly consumed with doubts and desires, outwardly presented the facade of a saint. The fact he tricked with no one, tried seducing no one nor allowed anyone to seduce him, at first annoyed *everyone*! Once it dawned on those around him that his posture was no mere deception, his godliness no intellectual boast, the Sunday services grew more and more crowded. The idea of a gay saint germinated and flowered.

Grimly, Mac came to realize James' entry into his life was, at best, a mixed "blessing." The youth *demanded* nothing, yet by his very absence of desire, he forced Mac into presenting privileges the older man would just as soon have withheld. The greatest sacrifice Mac was called upon to make was when, one Sunday, he stepped aside and allowed his assistant to preach the service.

James, unused to public speaking, started badly. Hesitating, mumbling, he was ready to step aside when to his astonishment, he saw Jake enter at the back of the hall.

James had decided some time ago that Jake was a scoffer, an unbeliever, if not a downright . . . atheist! If he could only reach Jake . . .

Concern for the handsome man flooded his soul, giving him a simple eloquence and grace he would have denied he possessed. It was the voice of love. The love of God for man, James would have said. The love of one man for another, Jake would have responded. As James gave way to his emotions, he carried the crowd with him. With simple, direct Biblical rhetoric, he moved his listeners—many, to tears. When he finished and sat down, spent and exhausted, Mac sensed *he* was the biggest loser of the day.

When the congregation thinned out, Jake approached the youthful minister.

"You certainly roused them! I wouldn't have figured you could preach so well."

"I wanted to give you something to think about," James replied gravely.

Jake grinned. "You did," he said. "You can toss words around. Fortunately you can't *force* an interpretation."

"You don't believe, do you?"

"I believe in many things," Jake countered. "If you mean, do I believe in 'God' and all the nonsense which goes with the term—no, I don't!"

"I wish I could persuade you . . ." James began, staring into Jake's eyes with an intensity only a Christian or cruising gay dares exhibit.

" —And I wish I could persuade *you* that religion is an absurdity," Jake interrupted. "It's an albatross fastened 'round your neck, stinking from the rotting flesh of every man and woman who's been slaughtered over the centuries in the name of 'God,' so you 'believers' won't have to face the harsh realities of your doctrines! The only way religion can flourish is in an atmosphere of fear and mental stagnation. Believers across the ages have maintained both in abundance. At whatever cost, by whatever methods!"

James was shocked by the vehemence in Jake's words.

"There is nothing absurd about Christ's love for man," he responded, using the sharpest sword in his arsenal.

"Love?" Jake spat the word at James. "If you can call Christ's actions indicative of 'love,' I'd hate like hell to see what you label depravity. I get sick to death of you people using the word 'love' to describe a dictatorship of slavery and death. Love is the one word you have *no* right using."

They might have gone on forever, two opponents locked in battle, titans struggling to possess a world destroyed, but Mac, watching the exchange, came forward. He greeted Jake with his false cheeriness and pried James away from the sullen man.

"Who was that?" Mac demanded, seeing an opponent and

sensing an adversary.

James told him.

"Well! I've always *said* you should quit that place! God's shown He needs you here! Besides," Mac added, practical for once, "we've done so well lately, I can afford to pay you something." Another concession!

James did not respond. He felt Jake's stinging words smouldering in his brain. He was not ready to give up the station job just yet. Whenever he tried analyzing his feelings insofar as Jake was concerned, James found himself confronting contradictions. Never before had he met anyone who so boldly challenged the *existence* of God. From the time he was old enough to understand (vaguely) the meaning of the word, the image of a vengeful God was held, clublike, over his head, and James submitted. It was like breathing, a natural, inevitable part of living. Back home no one even spoke of atheists (unless it was to denounce "atheistic communism"). It being assumed such creatures were mere mirages, dragged forth from diseased, unquiet minds.

Jake must be insane!

Jake, however, didn't look mad. Nor did he act mad—except for his disbelief. At the station he seldom said much on any subject. James longed to talk with the man—but away from the pulpit he was shy and awkward. Only God, directing his voice from the lectern, could account for the eloquence everyone later said he exhibited on Sundays.

James did not surrender his job at the station, aware that in doing so he *would* be sacrificing something. He realized, dimly, what he would be giving up. The knowledge made him anxious.

Some weeks later James and Jake were dismissed earlier than usual one afternoon. Jake eyed James for a bold moment then suggested, "Want to go down to the Spur with me? I'll buy you a beer."

"I don't drink," James replied, low-voiced.

Jack grimaced. "Afraid demon rum will make you forget all the precious restrictions your 'God' imposes! Come on! I know the bartender — I'll get him to dig up a coke — or are they taboo, too!"

"I wish you wouldn't laugh at me."

"I'm not *laughing*. I'm annoyed someone with so much potential is throwing it all away, following a nightmare dressed as a dream — talk about cosmic drag! I also hate seeing you waste your prime manflesh on that old fart you hang around with!"

James, pained, turned away.

Jake finished washing the grease off his hands. "How about it, godboy, coming with me?"

"Don't call me that. It's blasphemous!"

"Not to me, it ain't. Afraid to stand up for Him? Aren't you supposed to let everybody know the Good News? Shit!" Jake dried his hands and turned to go. "You coming or not?"

"Not there," James stated. Then, as Jake started moving away, James inexplicably hurried on. "Couldn't we go somewheres else?"

Jake glanced back. "Why? You want to try convertin' me? You oughtta run like hell from me, kid. I'll never let you get away with that bullshit. With me, you'll have to justify every fucking 'belief' you hold. You can't do it. The whole edifice of religion is rotten!" He shrugged his shoulders, adding, "We can go to my place if you'd rather. But I've got beer there — and I'm gonna have me one."

The notion of going to Jake's place filled James with more apprehension than the thought of the bar, but having gotten Jake to change his destination, James felt obligated in the matter. Reluctantly he accompanied the mechanic.

Jake's apartment was only a few blocks from the garage. It consisted of three rooms in an older home, sparsely furnished, exceptionally neat and tidy. It contrasted greatly with Mac's rundown, rather messy house. The wooden floors, waxed, gleamed in the pale light. A gentle breeze wafted through the place once Jake opened the windows. He snapped on soft music. James realized he'd not been inside any house, other than Mac's, since his arrival in Atlanta. The fact shocked him.

Jake returned from his kitchen with a beer for himself and a bottle of coke for James. He'd removed his shirt. His brown, well-defined chest aroused James. James understood too well what was going on. He wished he could halt the process. The only way he could do that, however, would be to leave. Yet he'd never bring Jake salvation if he ran away the first moment they were alone together. It was a temptation. James *knew* that. What he couldn't understand were his own feelings. He'd prayed during the short walk to Jake's apartment, asking for strength and grace, praying he'd be able to reach Jake. Now he found himself affected in a way which was not religious at all. He was ashamed of his weakness.

They sat silently. Jake on the sofa, his feet propped up on an old ottoman. James reposed stiffly in a chair, uncomfortable and uncertain.

"Tell me about yourself," Jake suddenly demanded.

James demurred at first, but after a second urging, he responded with words about himself. He ended by telling Jake of the incident which led to his venturing forth to Atlanta.

"Only God could have led me here," James concluded, with words uttered defensively, anticipating rebuttal.

Instead, Jake homed in on another topic. "How many guys did you make it with down there?"

"Why . . . none. Weren't none around." James was taken off guard.

"And I suppose you've not had anybody up here but that old preacher, have you?"

"He's been good to me—" James began.

"—Shit! He's using you!" Jake drank from his beer can. "If you didn't have such a passionate attachment to your precious Jesus, you'd see that. I oughtta seduce you—that's what you need, a chance to discover what sex is all about! Hell, half your preoccupation with *God* stems from the fact you probably ain't never had a decent orgasm!" He laughed. "I'm embarrassing you, ain't I?"

"Yes."

"Why?"

"I . . . reckon 'cause . . . I wish I were free to love you . . ."

"You admit religion restricts you?" Jake jumped on the words, ignoring the rest of the statement.

"I don't mean it *that* way. God expects us to behave as *people*, not like animals!"

"Why is sexing okay with *one* person yet taboo with two? With guys you can't say we're in the procreation business! Can't you *see*? Religion is nothing more than attempts by mortal men to control your thoughts and actions! Attempts by *men*, not some supernatural deity! By prohibiting sex, religious zealouts induce guilt and use it against you. For a *gay* man to sanction such lies is doubly disgusting. We're condemned because we *love* one another while 'God' is let off the hook for having 'created' us as we are! You can't have it *both* ways! If God exists, He's as responsible for creating *us* as He is straights. Sexual orientation is like the color of your hair or eyes, or whatever; you've got it from birth. We don't deliberately *select* it! That being true, religion is hypocritical for condemning us! What you religious nuts are against is sex of *any* sort! Sexual fulfillment is the closest thing to heaven on earth men can find. Because gay men know this, and understand *all* the ramifications of such an idea, we are outcasts!"

Jake's words alarmed James. "That's only *lust* talking. An existence based on sex would be banal."

"How would *you* know?"

"I'd better go." James put down the coke can and got up.

Jake sprang to his feet in a rush of movement which frightened James. He started. Jake saw the uncertainty and fear in his guest's eyes.

"Hey! Don't get nervous. I'm not going to *rape* you!" Jake advanced until he was so close James could feel the man's breath, the warmth of his flesh. Jake reached out and placed a hand on James' shoulder. The hand was firm and hard, calloused. James shivered.

Jake dropped his hand and grabbed James' fingers, lifting them to his lips. "You're beautiful," Jake said. "And I want you. When you get tired of that old man, you're welcome here." He dropped James' hand and turned away.

Back on the street, James found himself mightily confused. He walked slowly back to the ministry headquarters. Like most religious people, James, at heart, was desirous of doing what was *right*, because it *was* right. He had never considered the question of ethics apart from God.

What if . . .

What if religion *were* an illusion?

The concept formed itself into words inside his mind, conjuring up images of hell, visions more powerful than any of Dante's ravings. Yet . . . "what if" persisted. Tugging at the lid of his consciousness, demanding acknowledgment in a context *outside* religion. Even James was intelligent enough to see using the *Bible* as the sole basis for belief was like using *Gone with the Wind* as authentic history: each obviously contained "truth," yet the essence of the novel was fictitious, in spite of the fact the *war* it described was real. *Atlanta* was real and the fiery destruction wrought against the "Phoenix of the South" was factual, too. A cold shiver swept James. What if the Bible were only a *book*, constructed along the same lines as a novel? He suddenly felt a need for Mac's cheery confidence. On reaching the ramshackle house, he saw with relief Mac's old station wagon parked in the driveway. He hurriedly let himself in.

In the cluttered living room, on the sofa, James found Mac giving a blow-job to some arrogant young thing who was, at best, sixteen.

Startled, Mac tried getting to his feet but the weight of his overburdened stomach, shifting so suddenly, threw him off balance. He lost his footing and plopped onto the floor. His youthful companion, more interested in James, eyed the new arrival with appraising eyes.

"Hi stud, want a turn?"

James stood taking in the scene. It might have been a frame from a film captured in a broken projector. No one moved. With his mind frozen, James grasped the answer to many previously unuttered questions. In one swift, sharp, burst of insight he saw things clearly for the first time. Glancing at the youngman with his erect cock and inviting look, James declined.

"No. Thanks just the same."

He edged past the naked pair and walked down the hallway to his room. There he packed his few possessions, took one comprehensive look around the room and left.

In the office he phoned Jake.

"Did . . . you mean what you said earlier—that I . . . could stay at your place? I'd only need to be there a couple of days . . ."

"What's up? You in trouble?"

"Not . . . exactly. I just need a place to stay for a while."

"Sure. Come over. Want me to pick you up?"

"No. I'll be there directly." James replaced the phone, stooped to pick up his bag and, turning, found a red-faced Mac staring at him.

"Now James," Mac began in a light tone. "You mustn't misconstrue what you saw just now—"

"Not much chance of doing that," James answered laconically.

"B . . . b . . . but it was the *only* way I could reach him," Mac sputtered. "Not *everyone* can be brought to Jesus *directly*. First you gotta get a person's attention! Then—"

"You trying to tell me that was supposed to be an attempt at conversion?" James made no effort at keeping incredulity out of his voice.

Mac faltered. "Well . . . yes . . . in a way. *Everyone* isn't blessed with your gift of words, you know." This last, Mac spoke angrily, ready to attack, to get himself back on the offensive.

"Nor my stupidity either, I reckon. I'm leaving."

"Oh, come back here!" Mac barked. "You're young! You don't know *all* the ways of reaching people! You can't throw away your ministry so casually. God won't permit it! God'll get you for doing that!"

"Let Him," James snapped. "I may be slow, but I got a lot of thinking to do. Seems to me there's a heap of *threats* with God. I'm sorta tired of all that. I been thinking God and Religion was love . . . seems like I might be wrong. When I find out, I'll let God know. If He's listening. In the meantime, you old fraud, you can suck all the cocks you want. I'm going!"

And grabbing his bag, he left. It was, he supposed, as good an exit as any.

He wasn't sure if God and Jesus were leaving with him or not. Guilt stirred and could not be stilled. He remembered Jake's glance and Jake's body, the quiet dignity of the apartment he'd visited earlier. If God existed, He ought to be able to find His way to such a peaceful home—and if He were only an image etched on the minds of justifying fools like Mac, James wanted to know that, too. Whatever the outcome, a feeling was growing within James that the answer was *knowable*.

Without realizing it yet, James had already discovered half the answer.

# Transfiguration

The house, small and dingy, was situated on a lot at the edge of a little-used public park. Only empty space surrounded the property—as if other buildings haughtily had chosen to shun the pathetic site. A few trees, shrubs and a garden, carefully tended in the back, were the only indications of a hesitant occupancy. The scene shouted loneliness and isolation at people who drove by the forlorn dwelling.

Whenever passers-by chanced to intrude upon the man who lived in the diminutive house on the isolated lot, their view of him involuntarily sent a momentary spasm of uneasiness across the barren surfaces of their souls.

He ignored everyone who attempted to play the neighbor game.

Isolated by choice, he hugged his privacy about himself like a precious shroud.

Work took only the portion of his time needed to provide essentials.

He would have cursed any chance passers-by if any had mattered enough to demand the energy of oaths. None did.

Within Sanctuary, however, he grew expansive, animated and joyful, pleased with himself and his own company and only occasionally hungering for the arrival of Lover.

Lover. Who must come because it was prophesied.

Yet as he waited, he doubted.

Doubts, to him, were wearisome gnats, continuously battering his brain with thousands of imperceptible stings, persistent as Orestes' furies, they were. Still, he *did* control them, controlled them because he *believed* the next day's dawn *might* bring the Beginning Of It All.

Samuel wasn't like other people. He was shy and introverted, physically weak. As a child he had been severely put upon by bullies and other such mainstream folks as enjoyed a good belly laugh at those they decide to label unconventional. Samuel put up with their indecencies without acknowledging his martyrdom.

He *admired* their strength, while despising his own languidness, never dreaming he might somehow chance upon remedies for either. In the fashion of such timid, uncertain men, he drifted through life, stumbling from one crisis to another. At nineteen, his parents died and he succeeded to an aloneness which was absolute. He found a menial job suited to his temperament. Five years flowed past him.

On a certain Friday at six-twenty in the evening he was trudging tiredly back to the forlorn little house when he saw the picture in the boutique window.

The picture, a poster actually, was of an attractive muscleman, who posed proudly while flexing bronzed and glorious muscles. He exuded a strength, confidence and pride which seemed ready to leap out and attack flesh and blood foes. The catalog of attributes possessed by the figure in the poster were all those never experienced by the mouselike Samuel.

Fearfully he entered the shop, fumbled with the worn bills needed to transfer ownership of the picture and, having completed the transaction, blushed in an ugly fashion as he left. Discreet laughter from the snobbish, lithe, *pretty* clerks followed him out of the store.

Up until this time the only thing Samuel owned which offered him a modicum of pride was the sad-windowed little dwelling he had purchased with monies inherited upon the death of his parents. Now, oblivious to his surroundings, either real or perceived, he rushed back to Sanctuary with his picture.

Samuel had no talent for building anything; yet with infinite care, he managed to mount the poster on pieces of cardboard he found around the house. Then he hung it on the wall. It was the only thing on his walls, other than limp curtains which graced the windows' sad panes.

A simple act.

An act pregnant with a longing never admitted, acknowledged or shared.

Samuel leaned back on his bed and gazed at his acquisition. Gradually, over the span of some weeks, he began speaking to it, hesitantly whispering to the poster what dreams he dared possess in a world so alien to the visions which came unbidden into his mind. When he fell asleep, the man on the wall watched him. On waking the first thing he saw was the face on the poster staring at him. It was natural that Samuel soon was forced to give the man a name.

Michael.

Slowly, imperceptibly, Michael began exerting an unnatural influence on Samuel.

One evening, after lying on his bed for some time, Samuel arose. His leg had gone to sleep in the interval and upon attempting to place the limb beneath his body, he stumbled. He found himself on his knees before Michael.

His position in those seconds seemed so natural to the sensitive Samuel that he remained kneeling for some time. When at last he got up, he knew Michael was no longer simply a picture on the wall.

Had he ever been?

Michael was Saviour. *Michael* was God. *That* was what had attracted Samuel to the poster in the first place. He remembered the shock which had marked his spirit on first viewing Michael. He recalled the exact time of day. The moment of conversion — that precious instant when he *Saw*. When he *Knew*.

Christian Jesus never had appealed to him. Emaciated, weak-looking, a god-in-the-form-of-weakness. Samuel wanted none of that. God, after all, was only the image of men's fears. Samuel, with more rationality than might be expected in so cowed a man, wanted God glorious. He eagerly knelt before his poster and worshiped that most glorious God of all—Michael.

The transformation of Michael from muscleman poster to Saviour-On-The-Wall did not happen in a day. The osmosis was slow, but beyond Samuel's power to halt.

Just as unerring were the subtle changes the new God forged in Samuel. As the young man offered his daily prayers to Michael, he sensed God's displeasure with *him*. God, in the guise of Michael, was strong, virile, manly; Samuel weak, vacillating, incompetent—not a fit worshiper for Michael-The-God. Daily, Michael accused his pitiful priest with stern eyes. Looks which, while not unfriendly, were demanding, challenging, and above all, arrogant.

After his inadequacies were brought to Samuel's attention by Michael's unyielding eyes, the young man grew desolate as he sensed he was not even pleasing God. Gods *ought* to be satisfied simply by being worshiped, Samuel thought resentfully. He lay on his bed in the ebony satin of night, begging he might be *forgiven* his deficiencies, praying to be accepted *as he was*. Michael—beautiful, manly Michael—was unbending. Master over his abject follower in ways Christ (we are told) dared not demand, the new Saviour-On-The-Wall was adamant.

At last Samuel discovered what God was trying to tell him.

The message struck forcibly as he passed a sporting good store. There, in the window, stood Michael. A small inconspicuous picture of Michael was being used as an advertising pitch for weight-lifting equipment, but all Samuel saw was the rapture of God. For only the second time in his life, Samuel was *sure* of something. *Absolutely* sure. As positive of knowing the will of God as a Baptist spouting Genesis at a school-board meeting, he knew what he was being ordered to do.

He bought the equipment and requested it be delivered to his small house, taking no notice of the snickers his purchase elicited.

The day the weights were delivered, Samuel began working out with them under the stern, but now-approving eyes of Michael/Saviour.

Transfiguration

Samuel's struggle was slow, but the outcome inevitable. As over the months his body slowly and painfully reached a plateau of physical perfection, his character was molded to match his flesh. He grew sure of himself, confident. When he found it necessary to contend with other people, he did so with a new authority. His shyness and diffidence fell away like leaves from the limbs of frost-struck trees.

Fervently, and often, he prayed to Michael.

And, as is the case with Gods, Michael one day responded in a "vision."

God spoke authoritatively of duty, obedience and lastly, of love.

God in the guise of Michael promised him, Samuel, love! Not only *love*, but love in its purest, noblest form, homosexual love, love in the shape of a male who would be equal to the demigod *Samuel* had become.

Michael, as is the wont of Gods, contemptuously dismissed women. Soft, clinging women — as useless to divine Samuel as cobwebs in a musty corner.

Certain now that one day Lover would arrive, Samuel continued his exercising. At the same time, confident of his strength, his new power, trusting his Saviour-On-The-Wall, he oftentimes left home and strode the streets of City. Why he did this he could not have articulated since before he found God, he would never have dared venture into that primeval darkness — which was all life away from Sanctuary. Now, however, the very process of placing foot after foot upon pavement incrased his self-assurance, his eagerness, his just-short-of-demand that God produce Lover.

Produce Him now!

As mirrors showed Samuel an outward newness about himself, so, too, did an eager inner stirring grip the man. The muscles of his groin would tighten, even while praying to God/Michael . . . new urges smote the man reborn.

Workouts, showers, prayers, could no longer still the infectious flame burning for release.

Lover was promised, why came he not?

Samuel stalked City streets, wharves and parks, watching as hungering eyes devoured him. In *his* new-found arrogance, he dismissed these crude supplicants. Over and over he haunted areas where men, reduced to dim shadows in a night-world, sought one another. Lanes where passion was grabbed desperately by frightened males, each eager for one another, each fearful that the moment's spasm of delight might become a demand—an attempt to barter their vaunted anonymity into a pursuit of the eternal.

Walk. Walk. Walk.

Searching—until Michael stood before him.

"Goddamn, stud! Where the hell did you come from?"

Samuel stared, but had no words to throw at God.

The man scrutinized Samuel more carefully.

"Look. You *are* interested, aren't you? Hell, I've seen you cruising around down here often enough . . ." God/Michael hesitated. "Never have seen you leave with anybody, though. I . . . wasn't sure *what* your game was." When Samuel still did not speak, the man turned away, disgusted. "Shit. You must be a goddamn deafmute—"

Samuel, silent, pleading wordlessly, reached out and touched the apparition.

Michael turned. The scowling eyes flashed bright with final approval.

"You *do* want me, don't you bastard! Got a place?" In his exuberance at being accepted, Michael grasped Samuel's arm, friendly, a comrade sharing love, life and that desperate longing . . .

"Look at those fuckin' queers."

The words were thrust out, harsh and rigid, diseased tongues between the lips of punks and pigs, grim and determined, seeking in never-ending cycles of violence, to smash worshiper and worshiped, Created and Creator. Michael and Samuel turned to face an onslaught.

Horrified, Samuel saw God struck. The enormity of the sacrilege galvanized him.

The queer-baiters expected little resistance, even from two

such musclemen. Queers, by definition, were fearful, cowed, half-men. They might work out in order to look pretty, but they remained only manly *portraits* —framed in bronze and mirage; one solid punch against their sculptured bodies would bring pain, hence collapse.

The opposite sparked and flared into reality.

As he felt a man's fist smash into his face, saw his new friend/ old God struggle to defeat two attackers, Samuel experienced an awakening. The physical reality of fighting broke apart years of enforced personal reserve and stirred pits of deep-seated animosities stored like putrid acid over a timelessness of undefended hurts. He swung now-powerful fists at all the enemies of past and present. Joyfully, he heard and felt the crunch of flesh against bone; with new ears and first-seeing eyes, he moved and roared with the exalted passion of righteousness. Inside five minutes the ragged forms of their attackers disappeared back into the blackness of frightened heterosexuality. Behind they left a new Samuel, inhabiting a new world. The old Samuel and his fears had passed away.

God brushed himself off and tentatively touched his novice-priest. Seeing tremulous welcome in Samuel's eyes, God said simply, "Let's go."

The house looked not so forlorn  as two men now instead of one crossed Sanctuary's portals. They paused only long enough to scrape the mud of battlefield from torsos, strong and indestructible. With calculated slowness, two forms touched and grappled and worshiped at altars abundant and overflowing.

In the gray light of a new day, the first dawn of forever, both males stirred, eyed one another and rejoiced. Michael glanced about and saw the Saviour-On-The-Wall.

"Oh shit, man! You got one of my old posters!"

"Yours?"

"Sure! Can't you tell? I haven't aged *that* much!" Michael jumped out of bed and padded over to the poster. He assumed the same pose.

"See? It's me all right. They took this five years ago—sorry

67

bastards. Paid me a miserable hundred bucks! Made a fortune
out of it." In a savage motion of rage, he jerked the poster off the
wall. "You mind if I get rid of it? It really pisses me off."

As Samuel nodded his assent, Michael ripped the offending
picture into several pieces and dropped them into the room's
convenient garbage can. Then, almost diffidently, he said, "You
don't need a picture, man, you got me—the real thing. If . . . you
want me."

Samuel climbed to his knees and pulled Michael to him.
Wrapping his arms around God's waist, he buried his face in
Michael's flesh. With a feeling intensified by the years of denial,
Samuel offered a soul bursting with a love so strong it could, at
this one special second, encompass all mankind. He responded.

"I do, my Lord! God! You know . . . I do!"

With appetites unsatiated they fell upon one another, feeding
their undiminished passion. Had dream become reality, or the
reality fled into the dream? It made no difference, for in truth,
both were the same, stitched together from the same fragile
fabric of longing and desire for the unattainable.

# The Shrine

The South is changing. The years move too fast, the pace quickens and life in the region, influenced at last by that all-powerful eye of God, television, races to catch up with the world outside its insulated borders.

Yet not so long ago summers seemed warmer, families were closer to one another and crime was not an ever-present fact of life. Homes and churches could be left open around the clock; few people in those days were thieves, none dared desecrate houses of worship—shrines to the simple faith of honest people.

Henry Taylor grew up in those calmer times. Before the advent of turbulence, before evil was commonly broadcast at six each evening, Henry was already feeling a restlessness which would characterize the coming generation. He intensely disliked the narrow values admired by the staid citizens who were his neighbors—even the people themselves became symbols to him of a retrogressive stupidity.

Henry hated their smug piety. He grew towards manhood listening to never-ending homilies of godliness offered by the area's hierarchy of "Aunt Marthas" and "Uncle Johns." They acted like sabbath devotions were coupons—so many per Sunday. Snuff coupons or church attendance—each held a distinct value, both being highly rated. At the same time everyone's daily transactions, filled with sin and sensuality, belied the assessed worth of collecting Sundays—or was it that after so many Sundays' worth of virtue, one became entitled to an evening of sin?

Having little experience of the inconsistencies of human nature, Henry allowed his precocious mind the luxury of rebelling against what a decade later would be called "community standards."

The Taylors occupied a large house in a small town. The name of the little village is best left out of the story, since it does not affect the substance of the tale in the slightest way. The town might be any one of several hundred in Georgia, south of Macon. Slow and tranquil, with less than five thousand inhabitants to disrupt its placid soul, the town lay supine for decades.

Henry's mother was dead, his father well-to-do. The senior Taylor had two major preoccupations: increasing his substantial fortune, and whoring. The passing of Mrs. Taylor had been a blessing to the father. The boy's mother was understood to have been a fine, genteel lady of a type the South seems capable of producing in abundance. Such women are like gnats, worrisome but persistent. Brushed aside, they fly back in your face before you have time to drop your hand. Not long after her unfortunate marriage, Mrs. Taylor discovered the vile nature of her husband's character. She never properly recovered from the astonishment that men such as her husband could continue to flourish and draw breath beneath God's heaven. The consequence of having married such a man, however, was of less significance to her; she simply prayed harder—realizing she was being penalized for some long-forgotten sin. Divorce in that era was considered a stain only marginally less demeaning than having an idiot in the family—it was clearly not a suitable option for people of the Taylors' class. Besides, neither party wanted one. Mrs. Taylor preferred suffering in wounded silence, allowing her husband to evolve into her "cross to bear." He, in turn, had his image as a fine, upstanding pillar of the community to maintain. She bore him three children before obligingly "passing away," having first suffered the humiliating experience of becoming infected with gonorrhea from one of her husband's escapades.

Henry, the last child, was five when his mother died. His only clear remembrance of her was a perpetual frown. His brother was many years older than young Henry. They were not close. The middle child was a girl. Henry, in typical southern male fashion, never paid much attention to her. She took after the mother, adopting prissy, smug, superficially devout mannerisms. Like many children, she quickly learned which methods worked best for getting her own way and acted accordingly. With a brother so much older than himself and a sister he could not tolerate, Henry grew up alone.

Henry's father, always occupied with his two pursuits, obviously had no time to look after his offspring. The children were placed in the charge of an aunt-housekeeper who further delegated the care of house, niece, and nephews to a black maid. Auntie allowed herself the luxury of two comforts: religion and liquor. The pair might seem incompatible, but while under the influence of the latter, the former always looked more fulfilling. The aunt, finding Jesus in a Pentecostal guise, was able to perform better at services having imbibed a bit of God's Holy Water. She so moved her fellow-worshipers with her antics that they never bothered questioning the source of her inspiration. She was, after all, never *tipsy*.

Coming from such an environment, Henry should not be blamed too harshly for the somewhat unconventional twist of his mental and emotional character. Actually, insofar as most matters were concerned, he was a rather uncomplicatedyoung man. He had few interests, no hobbies and, other than a profound contempt for everyone in the little town, no abiding passion. As soon as he was old enough, he followed his older brother to the state university, forgetting, as often as he could, the disgusting place of his birth.

In those days, the fifties let us suppose, it was not always easy putting the past completely in its place. In spite of the diversity of the Taylor family, the elder Taylor, concerned primarily with appearances, felt he should occasionally conform to the town's vision and expectations of himself as a man of property and substance. In the old man's mind this translated into gathering his family around him once in a while, attending church with his children, and, in general, acting out the role of community leader to which his wealth and social position entitled him. In spite of the fact everyone in town was aware of the older Taylor's whoring, it was an age when "out of sight, out of mind" was taken literally. Henry never got over being annoyed by the hypocrisy of it all. The longer he allowed his mind to dwell upon the matter, the more incensed he became at the pretense, the cant, of the situation. Every time a visit home loomed before him, Henry began to brood. By the time the trip south grew into a reality, the young man found himself in a state.

The time usually chosen for these displays of family togetherness was around the holidays. Partly because this was the only time of year the elder Taylor could tear himself away from the wayward ladies he fancied  and partly because it was easier getting all the younger Taylors home at such a time to complete the tableau.

On this particularly occasion Henry arrived home in a more pronounced state of rebellion than usual, even for him. The circumstances of his agitation were unclear—but no doubt having spent the past three years in an urbane university atmosphere helped fuel his fervent dislike for the town of his birth.

Possibly Henry's attitude stemmed from the fact he had reached the age of twenty-one and was feeling his manhood in a more assertive fashion than before. But Henry's manhood presented difficulties of its own, for he was one of those rare and beautiful creatures, a homosexual. He accepted the beauty of his preference because it set him apart from all others—a modern-day Job, punished without having sinned. The rarity of his proclivity was just as readily confirmed; he had never met, nor heard of, anyone else who shared it. Like God, he was one of a kind.

Whatever the reasons, Henry's hometown now filled him with a relentless loathing. The Taylor patriarch ballooned into a larger-than-life symbol of ridicule. (Henry actually admired his father very much; the old man, in his own way, was decidedly unconventional. It was the town's *perception* of Mr. Taylor which Henry objected to as dishonest.)

Henry's opinion of his sister remained as low as it had been before he left for the university. His only surprise, as far as she was concerned, was the miracle which must have taken place in order for her to have uncrossed her legs long enough to conceive a baby. The first Taylor grandchild. Henry's brother, concerned with his impending installation as Heir-Apparent, was too busy to have any time for the younger man.

Henry, having little else to do with his life, had become the family intellectual—by default, it was true, but for all that, he found the position one of some promise. He was in the running for valedictorian of his graduating class. It was an age when intellectual achievements, while viewed with considerable trepidation, were never sneered at by those less talented souls who managed to live without benefit of mental prowess.

Most young people are insufferable at best, for many perfectly sensible reasons. A young intellectual, with a sound basis for his knowledge, is beyond all help. He must either be borne in tolerant silence or run out of town. Our young man was no different—except that, contrary to others of his ilk, he possessed the quality, peculiar to himself, of keeping his mouth closed, his knowledge to himself. Many reasons might have explained his forbearance, but the foremost of these was a plan he gradually evolved over a period of some months. Formulating his plan, as well as considering the logic behind it, consumed much of his time in the days just prior to his enforced pilgrimage.

Henry wanted to commit an act which would show his utter contempt for the narrow-minded community and its unreasonable religion which cloaked the village in a shroud of respectability. Like the dead, of whom only good was ever spoken, religion, with its syruplike sweetness was held to be above reason. It gradually turned into a molasses-style flypaper, catching and holding every unfortunate soul who touched it.

There may have been a degree of self-loathing in Henry's abnormal desire. Being a homosexual in the fifties—in the rural South—was an especially trying situation. Henry's contemporaries expected a man to be either Godly or venal, but never acerbic. Still, such an explanation should probably be dismissed. Because, if honesty is adhered to, it must be conceded

that Henry was very vain. He was swollen with his own impor-
tance and contemptuous of others who, unlike himself, were not
blessed with a God-like genius. A psychiatrist might have
accused Henry of having a strong contempt for himself (based,
no doubt, on a hatred of his origins, his sexuality, or some other
hidden facet of his personality), but during the time of our story,
the notion of exploring minds for irrational solutions was not yet
in vogue in the South. If it had been, Henry would have dismissed
such foolishness. He knew the whys behind everything he did.
He understood himself and his own motives even better than he
understood the world—and his knowledge of the latter was not
inconsiderable.

His plan, when it finally reached fruition, consisted of one
simple act: he would desecrate churches.

Once the idea was born, Henry felt angry with himself for taking so long in reaching such a logical conclusion.

Religion was as closely associated with the region as mom
with dad, or salt with pepper. Georgia and Jesus! They were one
and the same. The citizens of the community would have been
gratified by the comparison; to Henry it was a combination made
for scorn.

As an intellectual must, Henry long ago had lost his belief in
God. (Here, his reasoning was exquisitely rational: anything his
aunt believed was, as a matter of course, totally without founda-
tion.) To his young, eager mind, his neighbors' acceptance of
Christian doctrine was a pathetic farce. All those Sweet Jesus
fools. Picturesque old ladies demanding their Sunday mornings
with God—like addicts pleading for a fix. Each Sabbath in the
choir they cheeped with gusto gory hymns about being "Washed
in the Blood of the Lamb." The outmoded religion had so many
references to blood and guts! Henry could not help believing
there was a significance in such allusions, and although he
could not put his finger on what the significance *was*, he knew
intuitively it was something ugly and grotesque. How they lived
for their Sunday dollop of church! The temples of superstition
were so damned important to them! Their churches were un-
pretentious shrines, the focal points of the community, holding

the fabric of society together like post houses on an ancient mail route. They provided much of the area's social life, served as meeting places for young people in that ageless cycle of boy-girl pairings and were generally the most respected of all local institutions. Henry longed to soil them. *His* type of men would never be welcome at their gatherings! Christianity's hatred of homosexuality was so pervasive it did not have to be articulated. Even if no one knew of Henry's act, he wanted to walk into each miserable hovel of ignorance, hate and perversity and defile it in some appropriate manner.

It took Henry a long time to select a scheme which fit his requirements. No perfect method suggested itself to him until he toured the sites of his proposed desecrations.

Then, the shape of his dream burst forth full-blown — Athena from the head of Zeus.

The design must be sexual

Once conceived, the aptness of his irreverent conception struck him with all the force which total assurance in the rightness of a cause brings its adherents.

Sex — the bane of religion!

Religion — the bane of sex!

Two opposites, so close to one another in the passions they stirred, the depths of feeling they probed, were the eternal horns of a bull-god. Rooted forever in the mask of creation, they curved up, pointing perpetually at one another, staring across the brow of God as implacable foes, each a demon in the midst of the holiest sanctuary, both too blind to see their common base on the face of divinity. Like pointed daggers they were poised across time, deadly rivals incapable of acknowledging they were prongs of the same source. Henry believed using a sexual motif against religion would be like sticking his fist up the asshole of God. He gradually grew intoxicated by the perfection of his plot.

Religion had never been able to tolerate the sexual side of man.

Especially *Henry's* type of sex.

Forced to sanction what it viewed as vile, churches veiled physical practices with layer upon layer of proscriptions clouding, destroying and distorting sexual activity. Henry knew very well why religion hated sex—nothing could withstand the powerful emotional currents engendered by the clashing of human flesh—illogical doctrines included. So, in order to maintain its unnatural hold on adherents, religion, unable to stifle desire, invented guilt.

Let the bastards indulge themselves!

First the fun, then the fear!

Hellfire and damnation versus sanctification.

And, once lust was controlled, subverted to the will of God's Church, it would corrode and rot the soul of the practitioner by its very denial.

Sex, however, possesses almost as many variants as Christianity has sects. Henry wished his dreams of finding a man—any man—with whom to share his body, could become a reality. Together they might partake of one another on the rotting altars of each church! He reluctantly put aside the notion: it would have been an appropriate gesture—as well as stimulating—but he didn't know any such men. Besides, he only had a couple of weeks in which to implement his plan—and there were a helluva lot of churches in the village. How in the hell could a town so small have so *many* of the damned things?

The very quantity of the houses of worship presented difficulties. As soon as he arrived home from the university, Henry checked out the deserving sanctuaries. They included three Baptist, one Methodist, one Presbyterian, a Jehovah's Witness, something called a Christian Church (hell, weren't they *all* supposed to be Christian?), a Seventh-Day Adventist and three oddballs: the Temple of Light, Congregation of the Lord Jesus and the One-Way Fellowship Temple. He was staggered by the sheer number of them. They represented a lot of orgasms.

They were all open. Henry had no trouble entering any of the diminutive shrines to piety. Each exploratory visit passed smoothly. He walked in, knelt down and pretended he was praying—nobody paid him any mind. Most were empty. His footsteps echoed hollowly in the dingy shells. Without worshipers calling forth ecstatic visions of heaven, or answering for grim, personal hells, the churches were mere buildings—drab and pathetic.

He felt his groin strengthen, quicken. Henry was ready—his flesh strained to challenge their godliness. He was John Henry with a ready hammer. He would smash and defeat the steam drill of God.

Henry vowed he would return in the eternal ticks of night and masturbate upon the very altars where they laid their holy Bibles.

Long reflection confirmed the scheme within his mind. Henry's face glowed with the light of intense pleasure at the thought of preachers placing their consecrated lies in his dried sperm. Since the motivation behind Henry was one of ego, as much as disgust with his targets, the *solitary* act grew to represent a brilliant slap at intellectual slavery.

The mission—close to sacred in the determination it aroused in Henry—began.

So many churches!

One frail man, rising to combat the many-headed medusa, was incapable of performing his God-defying act a *limitless* number of times each night. A compromise with self, if not with God, must be struck.

Henry decided three, the number of the trinity, so perfect in its symbolism, would become the number of his nightly visitations. One for the father, one for the son, the last ejaculation a present to the holy ghost.

The best of plans, alas, so often go awry. The site Henry selected for his initial foray was empty; he opened the door and walked slowly down the dark, bare aisles. The church was plain, the altar a simple affair.

Practical difficulties arose at once. The altar was not at a convenient level. Henry had assumed there would be some simple way of mounting it, allowing himself to masturbate in a position which would produce the desired effect. Unzipping his pants, he began the process. Henry enjoyed solitary sex, he experienced no inability to perform—his sexual appetite was great—a fact which marked him as his father's son.

As he leisurely went about the act, a delicious sense of achieving something forbidden—and slightly disgusting—sustained him. Would he feel terror? Deep, deep within himself, was not some small prick of fear revealing itself? Might he not be Struck Down?

Was that what he was doing here? He questioned himself with clinical fascination. Did he expect to hear some hollow, booming voice thundering at him from the heavens? Cosmic vengeance slapping him into a servile surrender? He knew otherwise. He climaxed on the altar.

As he zipped up his pants, satisfaction, both sexual and emotional, seeped over him like the advancing mists of a dreary fog across a barren landscape.

Dark acts, performed in shadow, within halls largely unfamiliar, made havoc of his schedule. Service to the father rendered, the son's yet must be done—while the hour grew late. Which target next?

He laughed aloud!

Auntie's church!

The exhilaration he would experience the next time she started prattling about the damned place? Only he would have the esoteric knowledge of the dried stains on the altar. His private possession—yet no less precious for all that it was his alone.

His and the son's—as if there ever had been one!

The hands of his watch galloped towards midnight, hour of deeds most secret and foul. His scrotum felt full again, filled with fluid created for defilement.

The pentecostal church where his aunt and her friends imbibed the God-wine was gray and uninspiring. Henry cautiously turned the doorknob—and found it inexplicably locked. What the hell! Secure in his new-found potency he knew no *locked door* could defeat him. He walked to the back of the church and raised a window. It slid up silently. Henry scampered over the sill, carefully closed the panes behind himself and made his way to the goal.

Here his luck was better. The pentecostal altar was an elaborate affair, one which provided an ample platform for his sacrifice. He climbed up and positioned himself. Dropping his pants down around his thighs, Henry began arousing himself. Long, even strokes with a sure, steady hand.

With each movement of his hand, he could feel the captured sexual powers within his body growing closer and closer to their inevitable explosion. The nearer he approached climax, the deeper, more intense grew the nature of his act. Henry felt his mind slip into a strange, mystical state, one enhanced in a way he had never before experienced while masturbating. He was struck by the sudden feeling God might not only be watching but participating. Religion and sex—the most powerful of stimulants. Combining the pair into a drama of God-sex could become the ultimate experience. Henry was at a loss to explain what he was going through—but it made no difference. He was on the point of release. As he neared his limit of endurance, a noise in front of him penetrated his awareness.

A dim form struggled awkwardly on the floor beneath the altar, flung out an arm and rose up on bended knee.

"Jacob? Jacob! Wake up! We'd better be gittin' home."

Jacob, whoever he was, stirred, groaned and tried sitting up. The woman vacantly looked around—and in the dim, filtered light believed she saw her Creator facing her from the height of the church altar.

"Oh! JESUS! Oh my GOD! We didn't mean no harm. Forgive us! Forgive us! JACOB!"

Jacob tried adjusting his tired, sleep-filled eyes to the light, such as it was. He, too, saw something moving rapidly atop the altar. The apparition had wings and appeared to be flailing about in great anger. Tremendous fear filled the souls of Jacob and his ladyfriend. They believed the hour of God's judgment had arrived. Trapped in their sin, their voices rose, shrieking incoherent appeals for mercy. Panic-stricken, they flung themselves at the feet of God in abject supplication. Henry, climaxing at the moment the pair knelt before him, experienced not only surging bursts of sexual relief but also an unspeakable sense of exaltation brought about by nameless voices pronouncing him God. The emotional maelstrom into which he was plunged by the screaming voices and the discovery he was not alone, lessened his powers of concentration. Instead of directing all his discharge onto the pulpit, drops of semen flew from the height of the altar onto the visages of his fearful worshipers. Their screams of terror did not abate as warm droplets struck their faces. They believed sparks of hell were being hurled at them. Henry's guttural cry of release echoed harshly across the rafters of the buildings, reached their ears and was transformed into the rage of a righteous deity.

Henry finished his defiant act, yanked up his pants and fled the altar top. The prostrated couple moaned and pleaded for their souls. As silently as possible, Henry left the church in the same fashion he entered. He was just closing the window when the front door of the house of worship burst open, lights flared on and several people raced down the aisle to investigate the terrifying sounds coming from Jacob and the woman.

As it was past midnight, the activity at the church attracted attention. Quickly gathering his wits about him, Henry realized the safest action would be to join the people now thronging the area. From the way the couple had taken on, he was pretty sure they wouldn't recognize him—besides, the sooner he found out how things stood, the better off he would be.

The building was buzzing like a plowed-up yellowjacket nest. Henry cautiously ambled down the aisle towards the scene of his love offering. In a circle surrounded by startled, amazed townspeople stood his aunt and one of the deacons for her church, Jacob Benefield.

"It was an Angel of the Lord!" exclaimed his aunt in her loud, piercing voice. "We came a prayin' for a vision and oooohhhh Lord! God granted our prayers! You may be skeptical! You may not believe! But you can see for yourselves! Our very faces have been anointed with moisture from the hand of God! PRAISE JESUS! Droplets from the Throne of The Saviour have descended upon us! Ohohohohohohoh! Merciful JESUS! WE'VE HAD A VISION!"

Henry at first refused to believe what his ears heard. Finally, in total disgust, he turned and walked away. He couldn't understand how *anyone* would take his aunt seriously. And what the hell was she and that guy doing in there at this time of night with the doors locked and the lights shut off? As if he didn't know! As if the rest of the town couldn't guess! She was just like his old man. Probably drunk, too!

Humans, however, have calmly defied reason and logic since the beginning of time. Much to Henry's annoyance, the citizens of his little town did not for a minute doubt his aunt's pious story of being in the church to pray. Witnesses on the spot tasted the droplets—finding them salty. Sagacious folks pronounced them a form of seawater. Probably mist which collected on the wings of the Angel as it flew to earth from the Gardens of Paradise. *Their* church had been blessed by a Divine Presence. The drops of liquid discovered on the altar were quickly collected on a small cloth and placed in a bottle where they became a sign of the congregation's—and Miss Taylor's—State of Holiness. There were, of course, skeptics at first. But as time passed, more and more people began attending the church. Rumors of answered prayers arising out of visits to the tabernacle spread far and wide—the small house of worship gradually grew into a state-wide shrine, looked upon as justification of the community's worthiness in the sight of God. Some even took it as a sign the town would be the site of the Second Coming.

Henry was so disturbed by the interpretation placed on the events which took place in his aunt's church that night, he discontinued his campaign against the churches of N———. As time passed, he couldn't help feeling he'd been used. Whether by God, the community, or his aunt, he wasn't sure. None of the possibilities was pleasant to contemplate.

As years passed and the commercialization of the shrine grew, Henry stopped returning to the town. He even stopped telling people where he was from, since in some perverse way they immediately associated *him* with the *Shrine*. As he aged, he grew morose and uncommunicative. With money inherited at his father's death, Henry had no need to work and gradually became somewhat of a recluse, given to reading and studying what his neighbors called "strange books." He settled far to the north of his hometown and hid away from his fellow citizens. He was observed venturing forth only occasionally, usually at night. To pray, some said. Rumors, spread no doubt by malicious children and vicious-tongued gossips, hinted that he did more than pray in the churches he visited. No one, however, cared enough to bother finding out.

# The Man Who Followed His Heart

## Nineteen Twenty-Three

I dropped the reins and dismounted. My horse and I were both tired and the sparkling stream directly in front of us looked inviting. I let him drink, sparingly at first, before finally giving him his head. It was late; we'd crested the peaks in back of us an hour and a half earlier and now found ourselves descending into a beautiful, but isolated, valley.

"Well, Pegasus," I said, "this looks like a good stopping-off place for the night."

I was just getting ready to loosen the cinch on the saddle and unload my gear when a voice startled the hell outta me.

"Hi, stranger! That's a fine-looking horse you got."

I whirled around to see a young woman, petite, red-cheeked and golden-haired, smiling at my embarrassment.

"Sorry I startled you," she apologized. "The wind was wrong for alerting your horse—and I move quietly."

"That you do," I acknowledged. A closer look showed she was lugging a large string of fresh-caught rainbows.

"Looks like you know how to fish, too," I said, making conversation.

"You bet," she agreed. "Me 'n my brother live down there—" she indicated a spot farther down in the valley "—and I felt like something different for supper." She eyed me critically for a moment, then, apparently satisfied I was worth her attention, extended an invitation. "As you can see, I got plenty. Why don't you join us? We can put you up for the night. Don't get many visitors around these parts. It'd do Kyle—that's my brother—good to talk with somebody other than me. I'm Millie—Millie Webster!"

Which is how I come to meet Kyle and Millie Webster.

Millie and I walked down to the house. Like everything else about the encounter, the building surprised me, being large, well-built, neat. It had a large veranda on which a man could lounge late of an evening and feel very comfortable. When we reached the place, Millie pointed me in the direction of a large barn.

"You can put your horse in there. Second stall from the end's empty. Use whatever you need. He looks tired." I nodded as she added, "Kyle'll probably turn up 'fore you're finished—just introduce yourself, he's easygoing. Supper'll be a tad late, seeing's I got these fish to clean." She ran up the back steps into the house. I headed for the barn.

Pegasus was extremely pleased. There was ample feed, so I gave him a good rubdown, fed him and was looking around for the well to pull up some water when Kyle Webster came in, leading a pair of work animals.

I introduced myself: "Mark Bailey. Your sister found me down by the creek and saved me from another evening of my own cooking."

"And me and herself from another evening of our own company!" He smiled and I felt even then that he was an extraordinary man. Physically, he was big. Six two or three, with a long, lean, hard physique, honed to perfection by years of work. In spite of the fact he was dirty and tired, there was an aura about him I've only experienced once before, and that was with my brother. Kyle pointed me in the direction of the well, and I hauled up a few buckets of water, some for Pegasus and some for Webster's animals.

"Hey! You didn't have to do that!"

"It's good to move after riding all day," I replied and he accepted it. Hospitality works both ways.

Supper was a superb affair, Millie having as good a hand with cooking trout as catching 'em. While eating, we exchanged stories about ourselves.

"I'm an orphan," I explained. "Ma and Pa died in a flu epidemic when I was eight. My brother Paul—he's six years older'n me—and I got shoved into an orphanage back in Georgia. They split us up, seein' as we were in different age groups. Paul raised hell about that, but the folks what run the place didn't care." I grinned and added, "I reckon I caused 'em enough trouble, myself. The damned place always reminded me of something out of Dickens. Anyway, once he turned twenty-one, Paul took his share of what Ma and Pa left—he couldn't touch it 'til he turned twenty-one, same as me—and headed west. Last I heard from him, he was in some place called San Francisco . . . in California. I'm headin' there, looking for him."

"Good grief," exclaimed Millie. "That's a long ways to go! Are you *sure* he's out there?"

"Well . . . not exactly. Been 'bout a year now since I heard from him. But I sure was tired of Georgia and all that. Maybe California'll be better."

Kyle chuckled, probably at my innocence. Then they told me about themselves. He was thirty; Millie, at twenty, was a couple of years younger 'n me. Their father had died six years previously, leaving them the ranch.

"We raise cattle. Try growin' enough stuff to feed them 'n ourselves. Pa left us some money. He was an educated man and had other investments, so we're not as dependent on weather and market conditions as other ranchers." As he talked, it was easy seein' Kyle loved the place. Towards the end of the meal, a discordant note was sounded. After listening to him, I'd remarked, "Looks like your future's all mapped out! Must be nice!"

His face grew determined. "Well . . . not really. Only for a few more years, until—"

"—Kyle!" Millie barked the word. "We are *not* going to start on that tonight!" She turned to me, saying, "An old argument between us. Just ignore it."

I nodded, it not being any of my business.

After eating, Millie chased Kyle and myself out to the porch. He lit up a pipe, "to keep the skeeters away," he explained, and we talked some more.

That first, long twilight with Kyle, listening to his strong voice, the sound of birds and insects as night descended, affected me. I tried calming my heart, which started beating faster every time he looked at me. I wanted him; wanted his arms around me, wanted . . . so much of him! Life at the orphanage, however, had taught me the hard way that such desires must never be uttered—and seldom acted upon. Only with Paul had I ever dared talk about the feelings, and while he didn't share 'em (I don't think) he'd at least understood. Or pretended he did. I expect Paul thought it was simply a need to be loved; damn those fools who separated us!

Anyway, Kyle and I talked. Millie joined us for a while, then (perceptively) left us to ourselves.

"I reckon you gotta push on, don't you?" Kyle asked as the evening grew late.

"Yeah," I answered, "I don't know how long it'll take, finding Paul."

"A day or two make that much difference?"

I stared intently in Kyle's direction. All I could see was the faint glow of his pipe.

"Well . . ." I hedged. "I've been ridin' Pegasus real hard. I suppose it wouldn't hurt to rest him a couple or three days . . ."

"I'd—we'd—like having you, if you'd care to stay," Kyle offered gruffly.

"Okay," I agreed. "If'n you let me help out while I'm here. Both me 'n that horse eat a lot."

"We'll see," Kyle said, chuckling softly. "How'd you come to name him Pegasus? Seems like mythology and that orphanage wouldn't go together."

"They didn't," I said, then sat silently for a moment, wondering how much to say without sounding silly or like a sissy. "I found the story in some books that belonged to my folks. The director of the orphanage wanted to take my books away but Paul found out about it and pitched a fit. The director claimed Pa's books were irreligious, but our lawyer made 'em lay off. Anyway . . . I guess I liked the story of a horse that could fly away . . . not . . . have to put up with all . . ."

All what?

All the conventional crap they fed us? Fly away from their shallowness, from their fear of emotions . . . fly away and seek love with someone I could admire, someone I wanted in a most . . . "unnatural" way! What'n no way I could say all that to Kyle Webster.

In the silence of my remembering, I'd not noticed Kyle had gotten up and come over to where I was sitting. His hand on my shoulder jerked me back to the present.

"Come on, let's turn in. Daylight comes early."

Kyle led me down the hallway. Millie had left a lamp lit. Outside the room they'd assigned me, he stopped, eyed me curiously, but said only: "Hope you sleep well. We won't wake you in the morning. Sleep as late as you can."

Then he was gone, taking the lamp with him to his room, leaving me in darkness.

Somehow the days just seemed to run together. I'd been there a week before I gave another thought to Paul. The ranch was large, and even though the Websters didn't run that many head of cattle, there was a hell of a lot of work to do. Kyle said they hired a hand from time to time but couldn't find many men who were reliable. Besides, most preferred working in town or on the larger spreads in the area.

I loved the time. It was hard work, under a blazing hot sun . . . but oftentimes Kyle stripped off his shirt and worked naked to the waist. Watching his huge arms and back moving in time with whatever chore he was doing  was both heaven and hell.

It was during this time that I found out what was driving Kyle and Millie apart. Millie was seeing a young doctor in town who wanted to marry her. This was fine with Kyle, who liked the guy; the problem was that Kyle was going to sell the place when Millie married  in order to give her her share of their parents' estate. Millie wouldn't hear of this, refusing to set a date for her wedding until Kyle changed his mind. They apparently had reached an impasse, and Millie's suitor, James Bryson, was in the middle.

Still, the fight between brother and sister troubled me not at all. I was in love with Kyle, without knowing exactly what that meant or what to do about it. Millie, I think, seemed to hope my presence would in some way eventually modify Kyle's intransigence.

Was I so transparent? I don't know. The second time we went to town, however, I wrote Pa's lawyer back in Georgia and gave the Webster ranch as my address. Temporarily, of course.

One Sunday, after I'd been there nearly a month, Kyle and I found ourselves alone. Millie and James were in town for some fete. We'd worked most of the morning, hoping to get the hay cut before rainy season. The day was hot, and about the time the sun peaked and started the down side of the day, Kyle threw aside his scythe and said, "Hell! Let's take a break!" He glanced at me, oddly, I felt, and added, "You want to let's take a swim in the creek?"

"Sounds fine with me," I told him, forgetting for a split second that we'd both be naked. When I did think about it, I knew I couldn't handle the situation—but by then we were halfway to the creek and what'n no way I could change my mind without an explanation.

We reached the water, and self-consciously, I undressed. I tried keeping my back towards Kyle while at the same time looking at him. He was so perfect. His shoulders broad, waist narrow but hard; his thighs, work-hardened, were magnificent. I could feel my cock start growing, so I headed for the creek.

"Be careful," Kyle warned. "That spot by the tree is deepest."

I leapt into the water, gasping at the coldness of it.

Kyle joined me. Deliberately, I looked away. I wanted to see how big he was—hell, what I wanted was his arms warming me after this frigid swim, but that took more nerve than I possessed.

We splashed around for a few minutes, until the water thoroughly chilled us. Kyle pulled himself out first. I followed, shivering even in the sunlight.

Out of the water, I hesitated at following Kyle up the grassy embankment. He found a comfortable spot in full sun, laid down on his back and closed his eyes.

"Come here, Mark."

I walked up to where he was, praying he'd keep his eyes closed, and flopped down on my stomach beside him. He was half-hard himself. It had to be the sun's rays . . .

Kyle opened his eyes and stared directly into mine.

"Don't look away," he ordered.

Reluctantly, I obeyed, but kinda ducked my head. I was embarrassed without knowing why. I could feel my cock hardening and growing erect beneath me.

"Am I . . . out of order?" Kyle asked, hesitant for the first and only time.

"No," I whispered, knowing at last why he'd brought me here, knowing he wanted the same thing I did, yet scared to death something would happen to ruin the happiness and joy I'd had, just being around him.

At my "no," his hand reached out and gripped the back of my neck. He pulled me to him, kissing me on the mouth, hard. The stubble of his beard scraped my face. I'd never been kissed on the mouth before by a man. Like everything else about Kyle, it excited me. I turned to him now, both our cocks hard, straining to penetrate whatever openings they could find.

Our inhibitions (mine at least) fast disappeared. We rolled around on the grass oblivious to everything but our needs. After intense combinations, in which we did things I'd never thought of, I turned my back to him and found his strong arms slipping around me. I knew then, no matter how good the rest of my life might be, this would be the most exquisite memory I would ever have.

His hands played with my nipples, making them hard and erect. His mouth breathed on my neck as he kissed and nuzzled me. Finally, he moved one of his hands, filled it with spittle which he rubbed on his cock and my ass. The orphanage had taught me what he wanted, and I was ready.

Kyle was big, but after a few moments I was used to him. And he started off slowly, gently; by the time he was pounding my ass in unrestrained abandon, his hand had guided my cock to the point that we exploded together.

As we lay in each other's arms, sweating in the brilliant light of the sun, on the crushed grass and clover which gave off sweet smells, I could not help but recall, bitterly, how that fool of a director at the orphanage had forced me to drop my pants so he could "punish" me. And those other occasions when he'd made me "spread my cheeks" while he rammed his dick into me, all the while exclaiming how it hurt him more 'n me! Now that ugly memory fled, replaced by the joy and love I felt for Kyle.

He slipped out of me, finally, turned me to face him and we kissed, long and deliciously.

"I'm sorry we waited so long," he said at last.

"So 'm I."

"I just . . . I find it hard, sometimes, thinking about anything except Millie, and having to sell this place. I love it very much."

"Do you *have* to sell it?" I questioned.

He shrugged. "There's no other way of giving her an equal share. We make a nice profit most years, but I'd never be able to make enough here to buy her out. I know she cares for the place . . . but when she marries, her place is with her husband. James is too good a doctor to stay long in a little place like this. In time, the situation would fester . . ."

"What about . . . when you marry?" I asked.

He slapped me, hard. He wasn't playful now.

"You think I'd marry? A woman? I know what I want — always have. Finding it is — was? — the problem. You . . . still got to run off to . . . where the hell was it? California?"

"I'd like to find Paul . . . but . . . I want you. I love you, Kyle."

Kyle stared hard at me. Then his hand brushed my face. "I'm not a man who can change. I won't love but once. Don't play with me, Mark!"

I clung to him. He held me then and I felt for the first time in my life that I had all I'd ever want!

A couple of more months passed, so fast I couldn't have said where they went. We worked hard as hell during the day, and at night, after Millie was in bed, we'd slip into each other's room, igniting our passion, finding it never cooled, never diminished.

We grew to know each other's moods, how to work in tandem
. . . in *every* way we were two men in love.

Kyle *was* worried about Millie, about the situation concerning the ranch. Millie, however, seemed pleased at my continued
presence on the place, hinting, to me at least, that maybe I could
persuade Kyle not to sell out, while at the same time allowing
her to marry James.

What might have happened, I don't know.

Because during my fourth month at the ranch, I got a note
from Paul, relayed by that Georgia lawyer, begging me to rush to
San Francisco. He needed me.

"You must go, of course," Kyle advised me. He looked as unhappy over the prospect as I felt.

"I'm gonna go," I admitted, "but . . . I need you to come back
to. I love you, Kyle, I—"

He reached out a hand to stay my comments. We didn't need
words any more.

I left the next day. Pegasus, well-fed and rested, seemed
eager to continue our interrupted journey. My ass was sore from
my last night with Kyle, but my heart was as content as separa-
tion would allow—I knew I'd return and find him waiting for me.

## Nineteen Twenty-Five

Nearly two years had passed since I'd ridden this path to the
Webster ranch. Two years without a word from Kyle. My heart
was beating hard as I neared the place. Was I a fool? Probably?
For months I'd agonized about why Kyle hadn't written me. In
the end, nothing made any difference. I loved him—and only
hearing him tell me to my face that *he* didn't care would be good
enough. My heart had always been at this ranch; I was simply
following it back to where I'd left it.

I sighted the house. Everything looked the same.

"—We're going to be married and you are *not* going to sell this
damned ranch!" shrieked a female voice: Millie.

"The minute you marry, the 'for sale' sign goes up!" Kyle's
tone was hard and final.

A bad time to return. Nearly everything that had happened

since I'd left had been unfortunate. What was one more tribulation?

The front door of the ranch burst open and Kyle stormed out. He stopped dead in his steps when he saw me—but instead of the smiling welcome I'd longed for, he eyed me dourly, said sarcastically, "It's certainly not my day!" and stalked off down the lane.

Millie, alerted by his words, came to the door.

"Mark!" She rushed into my arms, weeping. Then, angrily, she started pounding my chest with her tiny fists.

"Why didn't you *write* him?" she demanded through her tears. "He loves you so much! He'd change his mind if *you* were here . . ."

Things were moving too fast for me.

"I *did* write, Millie," I protested, "many times . . . eight, nine, at least. I never got any answers; I didn't know what to think. Then . . ."

She raised her head then and stopped beating on me.

"Are you telling me the truth, Mark?"

"Yes."

"Then go to him. He loves you! He still does. Explain—oh stop looking so *shocked*! He's my *brother*! I love him too, and if he's happy with you, what do I care? You two never fooled me! With you here, James and I can marry! We'll have enough kids for two families! They'll just have two uncles!" She giggled through her tears and reached for Pegasus. "I'll put him up for you . . . go to Kyle . . . please . . ."

So I did.

I knew where he'd be.

He didn't turn as I neared him, but he knew it was me. I wasn't trying to be quiet anyway.

"I'm not interested in company at the moment." He spoke without turning. Didn't he trust himself to look at me?

"That's too bad," I said. "I am. I didn't ride halfway back across the damned country for this. Millie says you never got any of my letters. I'm sorry about that. But I wrote 'em. I wrote and wrote and . . . never got anything from *you* —yet that didn't stop me . . ." I'd gone as far as I could, looking at his back. I needed him so damned bad. He turned then, when I mentioned the letters. There was uncertainty in his eyes now. His face had softened slightly.

"You wouldn't . . . just say that, would you?" He'd wanted to ask if I'd lied about it and changed his word. I was glad of that.

"No," I told him.

The situation was awkward for Kyle. He's a proud man. He'd apparently managed to convince himself I didn't care, that I'd been playing with him, and I reckon that hurt him a lot. That — plus always thinking about selling the ranch — must have given him a rough year.

"You came back at an unsettled time," he spoke slowly. "Even if you — if we — were of the same mind, I haven't that much to offer you."

The fool! I went to him, then.

"All I want is you."

He accepted my touch but not with assurance.

"I don't know . . ." He tried changing the subject. "How's your brother?"

"He's dead," I told him.

Then his aloofness vanished. He was the old Kyle. Without a thought he gathered me into his arms, holding me firmly, saying, "Mark, I'm sorry. I reckon I've been thinking just about myself — and Millie." He led me to a spot where we could sit down. "Tell me about it," he commanded.

And, in spite of the fact that remembering Paul brought back a lot of pain, I obeyed.

"I got out to San Francisco — 'Frisco,' they call it — three or four months after leaving you and Millie," I explained. "Paul was as irrepressible as ever. He'd gotten himself involved with a couple of guys in a gold mine deal and they were actually making money on it. But another group wanted to buy 'em out. Paul and his friends didn't want to sell. I don't know, even now, all the stuff that went on. Paul tried keeping me out of it. I think by the time I got there, he'd regretted asking me out, because of the danger . . . if I'd heard anything from you, I'd have left then."

Kyle squeezed my arm and muttered curses against the Government's handling of mail.

"Things kept getting more and more violent," I explained, "and one night Paul was in town with one of his partners when some guys rode by and shot 'em. Killed Paul at once. His partner, Lee, died a couple of days later."

I stopped talking and Kyle didn't say anything, just held me, which was all I was wanting anyway.

"I straightened up Paul's affairs," I continued at last, "and even without hearing from you, came back." I looked at Kyle. "I love you. I loved you when I left and I still do. How about you, Kyle? Do you care?"

He pulled me to himself, then, our lips met in that bruising, delicious kiss I'd dreamed of for two long years.

"I still love you," he told me. "If things were only different with this business of Millie's share of the ranch . . ." He let me go, got up and started pacing about in an exasperated mood.

I laid back on the grass, watching him, at peace at last, knowing he was all I'd ever want. I'd seen enough on my travels to understand what sort of happiness I could have with Kyle.

"Kyle!"

He stopped pacing and looked at me.

I leaned up on an elbow. "There is a way out. If . . . you love me. If you want me as much as I want you—"

He dropped down on one knee beside me and slapped my face. "Tell me," he ordered.

I grabbed his hand and held it against my lips. God, how I loved him!

"Paul left me his shares in that gold mine." I grinned, happy with Kyle's reaction. "I sold 'em right before I left. I ain't rich, but I got a nice sum out of 'em. Enough, I reckon, to buy Millie's half of the ranch. If you'll . . . have me as a partner—"

I got no further. His lips closed on mine and his hands roamed over my body, igniting all the passion I'd saved for so long, delayed for so long, dreamed of for so long . . .

# Nursing Papa

## Nineteen Sixty

I've always hated the long twilights we get in south Georgia in the summertime. Dusk arrives and lingers on, full of heat, dust and uncomfortableness. They've always reminded me of those "twenty-four-hour days" we read about in first grade—some damned place called "Lapland"! Where the hell is "Lapland" supposed to be? When I was a kid, I thought "Lapland" was a euphemism for crotches. I always got the giggles when we read about the people of "Lapland" which for some reason upset my teacher, Miss Connors. Thank goodness our readers didn't dwell long on the state of affairs amongst the "Laps."

Those summer evenings grew worse once I returned from state college and took to nursing Papa. I'd studied English, mostly because I didn't know a damned thing about anything else and had no idea what I was supposed to do with myself. Everyone assumed I'd either work in Papa's business (Turpentine!—can you imagine *me* in Turpentine!) or go into the ministry. I was a priggish little snot when I was a kid. Anyway, Papa got himself hurt in an accident and was confined to a wheelchair. He'd always had a vicious tongue—drove Mama to an early grave, he did, always hollering at her about some damned something. Paul, my older brother, left home as soon as he turned eighteen and joined the army—never did come back. Sis, Margie Nell, married Deacon Bishop's son and they moved to Atlanta. He got a job there with some ritzy company. *No way he* was going to come back to the sticks and operate a *Turpentine* company! That left me.

Papa and I never did get on well. His idea of a son — of a man — was some hulking brute who cussed like a legionnaire and screwed anything in skirts. Growing up, I was a goody-two-shoes and *hated* women — back then they scared me. So I wasn't Papa's ideal little man. After his accident, Papa made me come home from college to look after him. He hired a nurse (always female and pretty) but *they* all went home in the evenings which left me with him on my hands — or, if you sympathized with him, vice versa. We never had anything to say to one another.

Those damned twilights were murder! I couldn't think of going out til I got the old bastard put to bed, and he wouldn't go to bed til dark. Too hot, he always complained. He was too stingy to buy an air conditioner. Not that the old house got that hot to begin with. What with the pecan trees around it and the wide veranda, it was pleasant most times. I'd wheel him out onto the porch and we'd sit there, watching people walk or drive by. Sometimes Miz Tompkins from next door would come over and sit with us. This was *not* an improvement since she was the nosiest bitch in the county, always wondering why I wasn't married yet. How she expected me to find time to look for a woman, even supposing I was of a mind to, with Papa to tend to, was beyond me. Papa always cackled when she mentioned me getting married.

Since it got dark so late, once in a while Miz Tompkins would sit with the old bastard so I could go "walking" with Lavinia Clack. Lavinia was the daughter of the richest man in town, so we were supposed to be socially compatible. I hated her as much as she detested me. Happily, she got shot some years later, in mysterious circumstances, but of course I was "walking out" with her *before* she died — not that *I* could tell much difference. Those walks were hell for me, having to carry on a conversation with Lavinia while at the same time trying to stop my neck from suffering whiplash every time a good-looking man passed by.

Yes, as Sweet Lavinia might have said, I was one of "them."

Now, it's hard thinking back to those days when homosexuality was something not only unmentionable but even—truly—unknown. But you have to remember my little hometown of Tilton was small and isolated. It didn't start growing until the interstate came through and that was *years* later. Nor, in nineteen-sixty, had television yet made much of a dent in the habits of the citizens. Most couldn't afford one, and a lot of those who could (like Papa) wouldn't have one of those "contraptions" in their house.

Stonewall was a long way away.

So I walked down Main Street escorting bitchy Lavinia Clack and eyeing every hot-looking man I saw, which was quite a few. I don't know how Tilton did it, but that town sure did produce a hell of a lot of studs. Not that they'd look at me—not then. But that didn't stop me! Whenever Lavinia and I met another couple, she'd stop and giggle with the girl. The girl's date and I were supposed to talk about "manly" things. What I did, mostly, was stare at the guy with rapt gazes which either embarrassed or infuriated him. This went on so long that, unbeknownst to myself, I became proud possessor of a "reputation."

Everything came to a head late one *delightful* summer evening.

It was a typical twilight. I'd taken Lavinia home and returned to Papa and Miz Tompkins, who'd twittered and cooed about me and the bitch til I'd almost run her off. Since coming back from college, I'd been known to be rude. The problem was, at school, I'd glimpsed a world totally different from the one I found myself in, and I wanted more of that one and less of this. I knew I'd never get anywhere, either in life or with men, where I was. Papa was keeping me from living, and I didn't know what to do about it.

Papa was more irritable than ever. Nevertheless, I undressed the old goat and put him into bed.

"Ain't my bedtime yet," he screamed at me. "Where'n the hell you off to?"

"Where the hell is there to go in this town?" I yelled back. "I'm going to sit on the porch for a while and try getting some rest myself. Go to sleep and leave me alone," I snapped and stomped out.

Papa kept a heavy cane by his bed, and I could hear him

thumping it on the floor, trying to get me back upstairs. The cane was his signal if he needed me during the night. I ignored it.

On the porch, I flopped onto the swing and pushed it into motion. The gentle swaying calmed me a little as I tried clearing my head. I just *couldn't* put up with Papa much longer! I could see my life—my youth (same thing)—gradually slipping away . . . I had to *do* something! But I wasn't trained to earn a living, and fleeing north to Atlanta scared me. I did have a little money, an inheritance from Mama. She'd always favored me; the others were already gone by the time she learned she was dying, so I got her money. It wasn't much . . . but maybe . . .

My thoughts were interrupted by the sound of the gate creaking open.

Peering into the gloom, I could just barely make out three forms hulking towards me and the house.

I couldn't imagine anyone coming to visit at such an hour!

"Ain't you 'fraid, Silas, sittin' out here all by yourself?" The question was from Jake Tompkins, Miz Tompkins' good-looking son. (No one ever found out where he got his looks from. She was ugly as a mule, and her husband wasn't much better.) I'd dreamed about him for years. He was just my age—twenty-three.

"What ought I be afraid of?" I asked. Actually, I *was* fearful, but I couldn't have said why.

Jake's companions, two other guys our age, came close enough I could see them. Duell Taylor and Mike Mathis. Mike Mathis was the most adorable man I'd ever laid my eyes on, either in Tilton *or* at college. I'd hungered after him since I was fourteen. He'd never come to the house before.

Jake answered my question.

"Hell," he said, swaggering a bit (they'd had something to drink, but I didn't know that at first) "way you run 'round town lookin' at men, wouldn't surprise anybody if some guys got tired of it and came after you some night."

"I don't know what you're talking about," I stated boldly and falsely.

"Don't bullshit us," Duell Taylor said harshly. He leaped onto the porch and sat down beside me in the swing. "You act so much like a girl, maybe you'd like to be our girl tonight."

Before I could reply to that alluring proposition, he'd put his arm around me and pulled me towards him, his lips brushing my cheek in a pseudo-kiss.

Obviously, I was supposed to protest and pull away. His strong arm around my shoulder, and the scent of his sweaty body, coupled with his lips touching my flesh, even in a gesture of ridicule, was more than *I* could resist.

"What you want me to do?" I asked, hesitant. Wouldn't do to let 'em know how eager I was to find out.

Jake sat down on the other side of me. Mike simply stood on the steps watching us. Jake grabbed my hand and placed it on his crotch. His cock was big — and hard. I'd found "Lapland" at last!

"Those damned bitches we run with won't let us have any. You can feel how excited they done got us — we need some release; figured you might be almost good as pussy." Jake said the words in a husky, harsh voice. It was then it hit me about their having been drinking. They probably were as scared as I was supposed to be.

I always wondered what would have happened if I'd said no. I *could* have gotten up and run into the house. Still, Duell did have his arm around my shoulder. He'd taken my other hand and put it down between his legs. Just where I'd always wanted it, myself. In all my daydreams when I'd been in high school, I'd wanted something like this. Of course, in those visions, we were *friends*, playing around together in some leafy bower, naked like Adam, without Eve. Even in those idyllic constructions I'd been the one relieving them, or at least Mike. Now, I knew they weren't viewing this visit as a friendly sort of thing. Probably, if they "remembered" anything afterwards, it wouldn't even be with pleasure. But I wasn't about to say "no."

"Y'all want to come to my room?" I asked, whispering, fearful of sharing their visit with anyone else.

"Yeah," Jake grunted. "That's just what we'd like."

So I led them into the house, down the darkened hallway and into my room. I had a big double bed, and for the first time in my life, I was glad of it. I didn't turn on any lights. I'd have loved looking at them, but figured they wouldn't go for that. To them, the episode was something to do in the dark, furtively, shamefully. They wouldn't even undress. I shucked off all my clothes and offered them my naked flesh. As Mike was the one I *really* wanted, I went to him first. He spun me 'round, put his work-roughened hands on my ass and spread my cheeks. In those days I wasn't knowledgeable enough to have any lubricant on hand, and I reckon they wouldn't have used it anyway. Mike had sense enough to spit on his cock, and that helped. But not much. He was so big! Large, round, throbbing cock, standing rigid in front of him! Later in life, I've always adored big dicks, but he was one of the biggest I've ever had, and I was a virgin that night! It hurt like hell.

I screamed. Not real loud, but enough to worry the three of 'em. Jake slapped me across the face, real hard.

"Shut up, you little queer. You know you want it. You ever tell on us, we'll do worse'n this to you."

I didn't reply. Mike didn't take long, and when he finished, Duell mounted me. His cock was smaller, but by then my ass was so sore I couldn't feel much, anyway. It was while Duell was on my ass that Papa started thumping the ceiling with that damned cane. They all started. Duell lost his hard.

"What the hell's that?" Jake demanded.

"Don't worry 'bout it," I advised. "It's just a loose shutter on the window, upstairs, banging in the wind."

"You sure?" Jake questioned. "It ain't your old man, is it?"

"No," I lied. "He fell asleep *hours* ago! Come on, let's finish."

So we did. Duell got his erection back, then Jake took his turn. My ass was too sore to say I really *enjoyed* them, but I was enjoying the situation. Every time they banged my behind, Papa would tap that goddamned cane! In the course of their switching around, I managed to jerk-off, so, in spite of their selfish natures, I got satisfaction, too.

Once Jake finished, they zipped up their pants and slipped out. Jack pulled me against his chest, hissing, "You say a word 'bout his, we'll kill you!"

'I won't breathe a word," I promised, "*if* you'll come back!"

"Damned queer," Duell muttered. "Tole you he'd like it."

Like unquiet shades looking for misplaced cemetery plots, they melted away. Only my sore ass gave evidence they'd actually existed. I pulled on my pants and climbed the stairs to Papa's room.

"You did so go out!" he accused me as soon as I entered the room.

"No, I didn't," I snapped. Then, perversely, added, "I was downstairs getting raped." Nobody believes the truth. "What the hell do you want?"

"Don't git smart with me," Papa barked. "And don't talk dirty like that. Some damn fool might believe you."

I handed him the bedpan, which was what he said he wanted, although he didn't do anything in it, then went back downstairs.

The remainder of that summer, I hung around the porch those late evenings, hoping they'd come back. One of 'em at least. But they never did. Whenever we'd meet downtown, all of 'em but Mike would look away. He'd stare at me in a funny way, but never said anything. Later that summer, Jake married SueNell Spivey and they moved to Waycross. (Miz Tompkins was so pissed about that, Papa and I were spared her presence for two whole weeks!) Duell joined the army; later he got killed in 'Nam. One fall evening, after I'd put Papa to bed, there was a knock at the door. When I opened it, there stood Mike. Hunky, beautiful Mike!

He eyed me uneasily.

"Got a few minutes?" he asked, diffidently but confident I'd say yes.

I said yes.

Somehow, leading him into the parlor didn't seem the right move, so we went back to my bedroom. Everybody had left for the day and Papa was already in bed.

Once in my room, Mike pulled me to him.

"Come here," he ordered.

I went to him and he kissed me full on the lips.

"Like that?" he asked. I dared only nod.

"Let me screw you again." He reached into his pocket and

pulled out a bottle of something. "I brought some cream; it won't hurt this time."

It didn't — much. Not that mere *pain* would have stopped me. He was pounding my ass, hard, going into me deeper and deeper when Papa's damned cane started up again. Neither Mike or I stopped, and after he came, he lay close to me, holding me. I could feel his heart beating . . .

"You oughtta fix that shutter," he told me gravely. "Gonna be cold soon."

I nodded. He continued.

"I'm leaving Tilton. Gonna head up to 'Lanta. Look for a job, look for a lot of things that ain't here." He eyed me intently. "You oughtta get outta here. Won't never amount to anything down here."

I shrugged. "I don't know anybody in 'Lanta . . . and there's Papa . . ."

Mike moved impatiently. "You know *me*. You need a lot of work done on you, but if you did like I tole you, you'd have possibilities . . ."

Mike melted away into the dark. I stood watching him for a long time. Then, resolutely, I walked up the stairs.

"Where the hell you been?" Papa screamed.

"I was getting raped again," I told him calmly. "And I'm moving to 'Lanta."

### Nineteen Eighty

The Spur, hottest leather bar in Atlanta, was packed. The climactic moment in their third annual "Daddy" contest was at hand.

"And the winner is," bawled the Emcee at the top of his voice: "Silas Tucker!"

Silas accepted the trophy gracefully and waved grandly to the cheering throngs.

"God, *look* at him!" exclaimed a bystander. "What a hunk of manflesh! Would you believe? I've heard he's in his *forties*! Don't look a day over twenty-seven!"

"Don't get ideas," retorted his companion. "Tucker's got a very jealous lover. That's him, standing over there next to the old geezer in the wheelchair."

"Why'd they let an old bastard like that in here?" asked the youngman. "He looks like he oughtta be in a graveyard!"

Silas, smiling broadly, left the stage and bounded down the steps to where Mike waited for him beside the wheelchair. Silas handed his trophy to Papa and kissed Mike.

"Hee, hee, hee," the old man giggled gleefully. "Always knowed you'd make a winner. Movin' to 'Lanta was the best idea I ever had!" He swung his reedy neck around, gawking at the festive leathercrowd. "Wouldn't never see nothin' like *this* in Tilton!"

Mike grinned at Silas and agreed: "He's right about that. But it's getting late; you'd better take him home. You'n me got a long session in store tonight."

Silas nodded and turned to the old form in the wheelchair. Nursing Papa was *such* a chore.

# A Time for Honesty

He couldn't believe it! What's more, he didn't *want* to believe it! If it was true—and he wasn't ready yet to accept his friend's revelation—then why in the hell couldn't Rick have kept the information to himself?

Roger Taylor gulped a swallow of beer too fast and coughed up most of it.

Taylor steadied himself, amazed by the way his hand shook. Silently he cursed the man he'd known for over ten years. Damn! He didn't know at the moment which was worse about the situation: the fact he'd suspected nothing in all that time, or the knowledge his friend of such long standing was . . . a . . . a . . . goddamn queer.

The very word itself, at least the word Rick Benson used in telling Taylor about the matter, homosexual, was enough to turn Taylor into stone. The designation had petrifying qualities, a modern Medusa's head held aloft.

Taylor was scared.

He was scared as hell. Taylor knew he was alarmed because he had that hollow, sinking feeling in the pit of his stomach. He was afraid when the news got around—he never thought about why it should get out, he simply assumed it would—everybody would think he was . . . like Benson. He wasn't! Yet his fearful feelings stemmed partly from wondering if . . . well . . . they'd hung around together so damned long! How could he have been so stupid—never noticing a thing?

They'd met in the university gym where both worked out several times a week. From there, they'd gone to having a few beers together, hanging out with each other, finally becoming roommates in their junior year. Taylor always felt they had a lot in common: sports, outdoor activities and . . . he'd always thought, women.

Goddammit, Benson *couldn't* be queer! Not after the women he'd picked up, the skirts they'd chased together — just no way! But Taylor recalled his friend's words and the agony returned . . .

Benson knew it had to come. He'd fought it — fought it for ten years now and he just couldn't go on a day longer. Even with the certainty that the outcome was a foregone conclusion, he couldn't put it off any more. It was getting harder and harder hanging around Roger . . . playing the straight game, wanting him so badly, loving him so much . . . and not daring to say a word or make a gesture which wasn't couched in horseplay. It was too much.

He'd always known he was a homosexual — known it so long at least that the origins of the knowledge didn't matter anymore. He'd even accepted the situation after a time. He never quite knew what to do about it. He didn't like men who fit the stereotypes of homosexuals. He had no idea how he could meet any others if others existed. He wanted friends, not some casual, embarrassing encounter which would only cheapen him. It had taken him a long time to realize his attitude towards sex and love was still regulated by his environment, was primarily a heterosexual philosophy strangling a man who wasn't interested in the life that philosophy upheld.

As he'd gotten older, he found a few books which helped a little; but he had difficulty adjusting to men like himself. You couldn't meet guys like you could women; things weren't that easy. The only places in the small university town for people like him were restrooms — and one porno bookstore. He wasn't ashamed of being a homosexual — to his way of reasoning, it was something which happened to him, like having black hair or gray eyes — but he'd be damned if he could stomach the grim reality of what was available as meeting places. So he refrained from sex. And started working out at the gym. Partly to work off excess energy, partly because he liked the men he saw there. He was always hoping something would happen.

But it never did.

Not really. He was too shy to mix easily with the others believing himself too scrawny, feeling he couldn't compete. Several months later, when his workouts had built up his body, he still retained an imperfect mental image of himself which hampered his actions. Then, too, most of the guys belonged to cliques. Unwillingly, he kept to himself. Until the day Roger Taylor asked to be spotted on the weights.

Ten years ago. They'd both been twenty. Taylor was handsome, rugged, rough. Benson never figured out what made them click together. Even after he'd whipped Taylor every time they fought or wrestled, it never occurred to him he was the stronger, the rougher of the pair. He was quiet, introverted, always following in the wake of the hurricane of action which was Taylor.

Benson loved the man from the beginning. And, having seldom indulged himself in any type of sexual gratification except masturbation, it wasn't hard retaining control over that part of things. By the time they became roommates, it seemed enough simply being together. They had separate bedrooms so the temptation wasn't overbearing. The worst part of the arrangement was messing around with women.

Benson had gone along with the pretense of being heterosexual for several reasons. He told himself at the time it was the way to keep Taylor satisfied, giving the man no reason for suspecting Benson's real desires. The explanation, as far as it went, was true enough. Benson knew he'd have done anything in those days if it made Taylor happy. There was, however, another reason for fooling around with women, one Benson wouldn't admit to himself for a long time. He wanted to see if he could change his preferences. Maybe homosexuality was a phase he was going through, something which could be altered. No truth in the thought, of course, but it gave him a reason for his actions without seeming to be quite the betrayal of self which he later came to realize it was.

Ten years slipped by. Both men moved to the same city after graduation. They moved into apartments close to one another. They went to sports events together, took trips together. Even took their vacations with each other. One summer it was backpacking, another time they toured the Southwest; went canoeing down a whitewater river—always something rough, something which pitted them against nature, against life. Their time together became a perpetual challenge to some deep-seated, unspoken criticism. As time passed, Benson felt the situation altering. Imperceptibly, his love for Taylor grew until it was no longer enough simply being the friend, the companion; he wanted more. Conversely, he accepted the fact nothing more would be offered.

They still double-dated from time to time, but as he aged, Benson slowly grew disgusted with himself for the deception. If he couldn't have Taylor, he could at least stop perpetuating the myth that he liked women. Gradually he gave up accompanying Taylor on dates. On weekends when Taylor took out a woman, Benson went his own way. A path that took him, tentatively, into the so-called "gay" community.

He didn't really know what to make of most of the people he met there. He wanted to like them, wanted very badly to help the "cause," both for philosophical and personal reasons. But, once again, he didn't fit in. They shared few of his interests. Their politics were strident and, to his way of thinking, irresponsible. He heard about a "gay" gym and went there for workouts, hoping lightning would blaze forth again, but he ran into ego problems. Discovering the place physique held in his shadowy world, he soon dropped out. Finally he sat down and admitted the real difficulty was his love for Taylor. He didn't want anyone else, couldn't seriously begin searching for another man when the face of Taylor was always in front of his eyes.

Were they close enough for him to tell Taylor how he felt? Could he retain friendship, if not gain love?

Benson reflected about the matter for a long time. In spite of their long relationship, they'd seldom *talked* much—not about anything serious. Mostly their conversations were a lot of bull-shit. That seemed the way men talked to each other. Joking, roughhousing, but never anything tender, warm or serious. Once in a while, over a few cans of beer, they'd venture comments about the "future." During these conversations Taylor always declared he'd marry one day and settle down. But he never did. Which was another factor weighing in Benson's decision.

Why *didn't* Taylor marry? God knows, he had chances enough. What if he felt the same way? Benson never allowed his mind to entertain that idea for long—it was too emotionally charged. The very notion of a lifetime with Taylor, with them *really* living together, was more than he could take. But just suppose . . . life was too fleeting to pass up the smallest fragment of a chance for total happiness. If there was *any* possibility Taylor felt as Benson did, then the words should be spoken. If the friendship fell, well . . . it was a risk worth taking.

When everything was weighed, the most telling argument, to Benson's mind, was the realization he *didn't* know how his friend would react; after ten years, the two men still didn't know each other. What *really* went on in Taylor's mind, behind his careless words and casual gestures? By the same standard, if Benson, as he had, could live with and around his friend for so long, loving him, wanting him, yet never showing either the love or desire, then obviously the perceptions of both men were distorted. Each was seeing what he wanted to see—not reality.

Benson didn't believe a man could ever know another person. *Knowing* another human being was like love, an ideal never realized. John Donne had written that no man was an island, but Benson preferred turning the phrase around: all men were islands—forever separated from one another, isolated, alone. Incapable of ever understanding their fellows. He *wanted* to know Taylor in every sense of the word: physically, mentally, emotionally—yet he sensed such complete knowledge was not possible.

What, then, was possible? Between two men—or two people? Honesty, at least. Love, candidly spoken, proudly offered. Whatever the reaction, it was a time for honesty.

Benson opened the door.
"Hi, Roger. Come in."
"Sure, man. What's up? You almost sounded *serious* on the phone."
"I was. I am. Want a beer?"
"Yeah." Taylor followed Benson into the kitchen which he knew as well as the one in his own apartment. Each got a drink and wordlessly went back into the den. Taylor sprawled on the sofa while Benson chose a comfortable chair.
"So give, man! What's on your mind?"
Benson looked directly at his friend. He'd gone over in his mind a million times the ways he'd start the conversation, but like all such mental gymnastics, reality caused his mental version to disintegrate.
The silence reached dangerous lengths.
Benson's throat, in spite of the beer, was dry. His hands, chest, were damp with acid-smelling sweat. Looking at Taylor seated in front of him, knowing the outcome his words would produce, filled him with dread. He dared not risk it.
"Uh . . . look," Taylor started hesitantly. "If you got something to say, spit it out. Far as I'm concerned, we've been friends too damned long for you to be acting like this. What's the matter?"
Benson still found words impossible.
Suddenly Taylor smacked his leg in disbelief. "I know, you bastard you, you're trying to tell me you're getting married!"
Taylor's insensitive words ended Benson's indecisiveness. He knew he'd lost but found the courage to begin in his friend's false assumption. If Taylor really thought such a thing, they had no basis for a friendship in the first place.
"No. That's not what I wanted to tell you." His anger, the vast, numbing disappointment which was spreading over him, caused him to speak sharply.
"Oh. Well . . . sorry. I just couldn't think of anything else that'd make you act so fuckin' stupid."
"I've known you ten years, Roger. In all that time, we've never

had a conversation which wasn't mostly sports or something of no consequence. We don't know each other, probably never have. You obviously don't understand a damned thing about me —"

"What the hell is this all about?" Taylor interrupted. "You're weird! You're beating all around whatever you're tryin' to say. I'm not much on words, but hell, we've bounced around together a long time. If you got a problem, I'll help if I can — but tell me what's going on. Plain — not with a lot of fancy bullshit."

"Okay. I'm trying to tell you I'm a homosexual."

Neither man ever forgot that moment.

Benson, uttering the words, felt both a tremendous loss and a sense of freedom he knew would never be repeated. He recognized, for the first time in the relationship, there was honesty between them. The gulf of longing and deception which had separated the men was gone.

Taylor, however, was gaping like a drowning man, one suddenly caught up in a flash flood, capable of no protest, no saving action, able only to watch helplessly as the waters swirled towards him, racing forward with death and destruction. Everything in Taylor's world fell out of focus. For almost the first time in his life, he experienced fear. As soon as the words printed their message on his brain, he grew afraid. Nothing in his world, nor his experience, prepared him for his friend's revelation. People didn't say such things, for Christ's sake! As soon as Benson's words sank in, Taylor felt guilty by association.

"You can't be serious! I don't believe it — you're drunk! Or crazy! Or something!"

"No. For the first time in a very long time, I guess I'm at ease with myself. I never wanted you not to know —"

"Goddamn! I . . . why tell me? I don't believe it . . . but what the hell! If you just hadn't told me . . ."

"I . . . I might have somebody moving in with me," Benson floundered desperately with the beginnings of a lie to provide an explanation. "It would be obvious which way my preferences —"

"Shit! You're gonna set up housekeeping with a queer? With a guy? Why —"

Benson suddenly was fed up. He exploded his words at Taylor.

"No! Goddammit, I'm through with lies! The *real* reason I told you is . . . I . . . love you—shut up! I reckon I always have. Lately it's been too damned hard being around you, putting up with all the bullshit. *Pretending* all the time! I just got too goddamned tired of *pretending*! Being pals, the whole macho bit. You won't be wanting to see me anymore, I reckon—but I can't do anything about that. That's your problem. But you're great, man! It's gotten impossible being around you and not letting you know . . . I'm sorry . . ." Benson started an apology but suddenly changed his tone. More decisively, he declared, "I'm sorry—but only because you feel the way you do." Softer, "I'm not sorry about loving you. I *had* to tell you—even if your reaction *is* the disgust I expected."

"You couldn't think I'd approve! My God! What will people think! Hell, they'll think I'm queer just because you—"

"The word is homosexual, not queer. If you're going to call me names, Roger, make sure they're the right names."

"Man! I gotta get out of here!" And he left.

The situation remained unchanged for weeks. Benson realized he'd seen the last of his friend. His days without the supporting phone calls and visits from Taylor were tedious, hard. Painful. A thousand times a day he mentally kicked himself for having said anything. On the other hand, he always came back to the fact that his life was no longer a deception. He was happier having revealed his homosexual nature.

At least—that's what he told himself.

He reached the point of expecting nothing when, one night, his phone rang. He answered it casually, no longer expecting Taylor.

"Rick?"

"Yeah—Roger?"

"Uh, look. I'm sorry I walked out. I couldn't take it in I guess. You been okay?"

"Yeah. I'm fine. You?"

"Huh-uh." Silence filled the wire.

Taylor gripped the phone tightly, wiped his forehead with a sweaty palm.

"Can I come over?"

"Sure."

And they were back together in the familiar apartment, warily watching each other. With beer again. Taylor spoke.

"I thought about what you said, about us not knowing each other. I reckon we didn't—don't—I mean, I don't want to piss you off or anything, but I don't see how you . . . could want to make it with a guy—not after the women you had. And what you do, for Christ's sake—I mean sucking . . ."

Ignoring the latter part of the statement, Benson tried explaining.

"The women were just a way of keeping you at ease. I screwed 'em, sure. I can *function* with women, but that's all it is—a performance. I don't enjoy it. I didn't . . . want you knowing the truth . . . that was the only reason I bothered with 'em at all."

"You went to all that trouble because you . . . liked me?"

"Yes.

"And all the time, you didn't want a woman? You . . . wanted to do it with . . . me?"

Hesitation. Then, "Yes."

"Well . . . I gotta admit, I've missed having you around. We've always gotten along okay. I won't make any promises, but I reckon if I was drunk enough sometime, we could . . . I mean . . ."

"I wouldn't do it that way—not with you, Roger. Look. Just because I care for you, yes, even want you, doesn't mean I'm going to attack you every time we're together. I never anticipated having sex with you—not really. But as friends, I couldn't keep pretending I was something I'm not. If we go on hanging around together, you get used to the fact I'm a homosexual—" He noticed Taylor's grimace at the word "—and if you're ever interested and sober, fine. I'd love to make it with you. Very much. But it isn't *essential*. The important thing was not lying to you any more about something so significant. You can't imagine what it's like keeping such a secret from people you care for deeply. That was what I rebelled at—"

"I think I see. Look—let's talk about something else, can we? I'm not comfortable with all this. Hell, I doubt I'll ever be comfortable with it. Maybe one day . . ."

"Sure!" agreed Benson positively, joyfully.

They began going over the current baseball standings.

# The Man Who Stood in the Corner

I tend bar at the Spur, the hottest macho bar in Atlanta. After almost four years of poppin' tops of long-necks, I guess you could say I've seen every hunky-looking number in the city—and made it with nearly all of 'em.

It's a great life, believe me! Hundreds—make that thousands—of men pass before my eyes every night. I've got prime flesh myself, score all the time and have easy access to all the booze, pills and pot I could ever use. I'd hate like hell givin' it up. Once in a while, however, things happen that rock the boat. Incidents which make me wonder if I *do* have the best of all possible worlds.

One episode that jolted me into a vague uneasiness about myself involved a guy I started callin' The Man Who Stood in the Corner.

His name was Hawkins—but I didn't learn who he was until long after I'd begun takin' an interest in him.

He used to come into the Spur *every* Friday and Saturday nights. Nothin' odd about that—we got hundreds of regulars—but he was different. Never said much, would order a beer then take it and go lounge in the corner. He always showed up at the same time: nine-thirty on the dot. Way too early for a guy with looks like this one. Nothin' starts happenin' at the Spur 'til after midnight—and come eleven-thirty, this stud'd leave! Once in a while, if someone spoke to him, he'd be a minute or two late in takin' off. He was invariably polite. I never saw him react brusquely towards anyone. No matter how ugly or undesirable a guy it might be.

Hawkins was sure no troll, believe me! He was one super-lookin' piece of manflesh! And I wanted him. Wanted him bad. I'd have stayed celibate for a week if he'd gone with me. Well . . . make that three days—no sense in going overboard.

Anyway, since he came in so early, I had lots of time to observe him. Most of the time, at that hour, he was the best-lookin' dude in the bar. Outside of myself, of course.

He'd stand there at ease, leanin' against the wall. Not provocatively; he never actively cruised anyone. I always made it a point to serve him myself. After I got familiar with his face, I tried talkin' to him, but it never did me much good. Oh, he'd grin in a kinda shy way, mumble a few words, then head for his favorite corner.

God, was he a hot number!

After he'd been comin' to the Spur three or four months, I started clearin' away the few empty bottles in his area just to get a good look at him before he left. He always noticed me—hell, everybody in the bar knew I wanted him. I reckon he did, too, but he wasn't interested in me—didn't appear interested in anybody.

A few more months sped by. After I figured out I couldn't make him give me a tumble, I kinda ignored him for a while. That didn't do any good either, so finally I went back to bein' pleasant. I wonder if he ever noticed? Anyway, much as it galled me, I put aside the notion of makin' it with him. I was scorin' every night anyway—it got to where I was happy just seein' him in the place. Like walkin' downtown and lookin' at familiar buildings. He was there, life was all as it should be.

Not that I pretended to *understand* where in the hell he was comin' from. I've never been one to put off pleasure, but it takes all kinds. Whenever I thought about Hawkins, seriously, which was something I almost never do (think, I mean), I always recalled another guy I picked up a couple of years ago. Roy, his name was. He's always stuck out in my mind. He was an amateur body-builder—goodlookin' piece of meat! He lived some seventy miles

outside 'Lanta and came over once or twice a month. I took off
early one Saturday night just to take him home with me. After we
finished sexin' and were talkin' I asked how come he didn't
move into the city. With his body, he could have made it with
guys any day of the week. His answer kinda shook me. Said it
wouldn't be as much fun seein' so many studs together, lovin'
each other, makin' out, if it were commonplace. The way he did
it, there was an eternal awe about nights in the city. A purity
and innocence he knew he couldn't retain if he moved to the
city. I thought he was sorta nuts, but he sure was sexy. Anyway,
when I thought about Hawkins, I figured maybe he was like this
Roy—only interested in sex at some specific interval; once a
year or something. Some guys are just plain *weird*!

I reckon it was luck which finally flung me the answer. But I
wish to hell I'd never found out. At least, not the way I did.

It was a Friday. I'd stepped out for a quick smoke before the
rush started. Right at eleven-thirty it was. Hawkins had just put
down his bottle and was buttonin' up his coat. I paid him no
mind; by now he was a fixture and I'd given up any hopes of
ballin' with him. I'd just reached the back parkin' lot and lit up
when all of a sudden shots rang out. Like a damned fool I ran
'round to the front of the Spur—just in time to see a carload of
queer-bashers racin' off.

Four guys lay on the sidewalk.

The next half-hour was one of the most confusin' and hellish
I've ever lived through. I ran inside, shouted at the guys behind
the bar to call an ambulance and the cops, then rushed back out
to see if I could do anything. One guy was already dead. A
couple of others were wounded, but not critically. When I
reached the fourth figure, I saw it was Hawkins. My Man in the
Corner. I thought my heart would stop. I dropped down on one
knee beside him. He was badly hurt, but not dead. He tried
moving.

"Lie still," I cautioned him. "Help's on the way. Just lie still."

He didn't seem to hear me—or if he did, the words didn't reg-
ister. He grabbed my arm in a hard, vicious grip. I felt then he
was dying.

"Dennis," he gasped.

My name's Ken, but if he wanted me to be "Dennis," I'd sure as hell be "Dennis."

"Take it easy, man," I whispered, tryin' to quiet him.

He turned his face towards me. Wherever he'd been hit, the bullets all missed his face. His features, though pale, were heroically handsome.

"I waited," he gasped, struggling for breath. "I knew . . . you'd come back one night, Dennis. I waited . . . just like I promised I . . . would."

By this time the cops and medics had arrived. They quickly bundled the wounded into waiting ambulances. Just as they reached me and Hawkins, he spoke again.

"Tell . . . Dennis I waited. Tell him . . . Hawkins . . . loved him."

"I'll tell him, man, I'll tell him."

He needed the words from me. His need was the only reason I spoke 'em. How the hell would I ever recognize "Dennis" in the first place? They loaded Hawkins into the van and in a minute the siren wailed him away into the night.

I cried.

I was scared, shook-up, angry. I was a whole lot of things that night. My hand was sticky. Lookin' down I saw his blood was coverin' my fingers. I wiped it off with my handkerchief. I still got that rag, with his dried blood on it. Crazy!

Over the next couple of days I called the hospital, askin' about him. Each time he was listed as critical. Then, like always, I got busy and he kinda slipped my mind.

Well . . . he didn't, *really*. But what was I supposed to do? I didn't want to be involved.

Later, somebody, I don't know who, told me he'd died. Stories about the shooting always listed two fatalities.

And that shoulda been the end of the story—only it wasn't.

Some months went by—six or seven I guess.

One Friday evening, nine-thirty, I'm tending bar and this good-lookin' dude walks in. He ordered a beer and headed for Hawkins' corner.

That's what that section of the bar was to me—Hawkins' Corner.

The first weekend this guy stood there, nothing registered. He was just one more stud amongst hundreds. But he wasn't a man you forgot. The following Friday he was back. And the next. It made my flesh crwl.

And suddenly, I knew!

I walked up to him the next Friday, after he'd settled himself into the corner.

"Are . . . you Dennis?" I asked, more afraid than I'd ever been before.

He eyed me with grave suspicion.

"Yeah," he answered, after a dark silence.

"Are . . . you waitin' for Hawkins?" I asked diffidently.

I wasn't prepared for his reaction. He grabbed my arm violently, pulled me towards him and leaned into my face. I'm no weakling, but he handled me like I was nothing. I was scared as hell.

"What the fuck do you know about Hawkins?" he demanded.

Hesitantly, I stammered out the details about the shooting and delivered Hawkins' message.

He released me then. His face took on a sort of glow when I told him Hawkins loved him.

I never in my life believed I'd ever see love. I reckon I'm too cynical. Too much of a whore. But that night on Dennis' face, I knew for the first and only time in my life, what love meant. For one brief span of time—seconds—I saw clearly the chasm between what I had and what I might someday find, if I'd only look.

"Thanks, man. I appreciate the message. But he ain't dead. I'd feel it if'n he was." He didn't say any more and I started to turn away. "You don't mind if I keep waiting, do you?" he asked me softly. "Hawk'll make it in one day."

I shook my head. I couldn't have said a word—not if my life depended on it.

I went back to the bar, opened a beer and poured myself a double shot of schnapps. I couldn't stand it. Eleven-thirty came and Dennis left.

But he was back the next weekend. And the one after that. He was becoming a fixture just like Hawkins. I couldn't stand it.

## The Man Who Stood in the Corner

After a few joints and some booze, I'd mock his devotion amongst my friends. We'd giggle about it. Life was too short to waste it bein' "faithful" to a fuckin' *memory*! Hell, love ain't possible between livin' flesh and blood. Spare me ghosts! I conveniently forgot the look I'd seen on Dennis' face. I've always hated the notion of faithfulness. Our attempts at it are just one more way of tryin' to justify ourselves, adoptin' hetero patterns, pretendin' we're more'n we are. I started trickin' more than ever—two, three studs a night. The only times I wasn't screwin' was when I caught VD. And I only let that put me out of commission a few days.

I got to where I dreaded weekends at the Spur.

Whenever nine-thirty neared, I'd get nervous—and stay that way til the bastard left.

I began usin' more and more dope, stayin' higher 'n a kite while he was there.

One Friday I was spacier than usual. He'd come in right on time. Got his beer and stood himself in the fuckin' corner. I tried hard not to notice him. I worked the counter on the side farthest from him. The place began fillin' up, and I sensed, with relief, that eleven-thirty was at hand.

I wished to God he'd go somewhere else for his wake!

Irritated, I turned to the corner.

No. I was seein' things. I HAD TO BE SEEIN' THINGS!

Dennis, his eyes shinin' (even in that dim light, and me behind the bar, I could tell they were shinin'—eyes bright as the devil's) was talkin' to a guy—who looked exactly like Hawkins!

They grasped one another. Dennis pulled the man towards him and they kissed fervently. Then, arm in arm, they walked towards the exit.

I tossed my towel aside and hurriedly followed them, my head spinnin' like a planet. I *couldn't* be seein' what my eyes were showin' me. *Just no fuckin' way!* I don't believe in spooks; there *had* to be some logical explanation.

By the time I got outside, they were a fair ways up the street, holdin' hands, oblivious to anything except each other.

"Dennis?" I called after them. I think I called.

He half-turned. Lifting his arm in a friendly farewell, his words floated back down the street to me.

"Thanks, man! Told you he'd make it back."

Still clinging together, they disappeared up the dimly lit avenue. Their masculine silhouettes meshed in my mind, a searing vision of perfection.

Somehow I got through work that night. I laid off everything for a few days after that. I was confused. Had I hallucinated? I was willin' to accept *any* explanation except the reality of havin' seen those guys together.

The next week, Dennis was absent from his corner.

And the week after that.

Neither man ever appeared again in the Spur.

I was jolted into stark sobriety—for a nearly a month.

Gradually, I put the experience behind me. I took up drinkin' and pill-poppin' again, though never as heavy as before. Every Friday at nine-thirty, I'd always stare into that corner, wonderin' . . . halfway hopin' I'd see a man standin' there . . .

# A Picture of Rex

"Goddamn son-of-a-bitch," I thought. "Answer your fuckin' phone!"

I could hear it ringing, then he did answer, but when the operator asked if he'd accept a collect call, he refused.

I hung up. Pissed as hell. At him, at myself, at my whole fuckin' situation.

Another eight days and I'll be outta this damned place. Prison ain't no fun, in spite of all the gay shit that's supposed to go on in the joint. Sex ain't no fun when it's forced—at least not if it's forced *before* you like or trust a dude.

What am I doin' in here? That ain't none of your business and ain't got nothin' to do with this story . . . I've spent three years, eleven months and . . . I forget how many fuckin' days in this hole and I got eight days now to find someplace to crash when I get released. I was hopin' this dude—Rex Wilson, his name is—might be obligin'. I found his name in a sex ad magazine . . . he was one of the few in the rag runnin' a picture. About the only one I felt I could stand makin' it with . . . Wilson's a hunky lookin' guy . . . if'n the damned picture ain't ten years old!

He was also the only one who answered my letter. I bet I've wrote a hundred guys . . . this Wilson was the only one who replied . . . said he couldn't get involved with guys in "correctional institutions"! Fuckin' smartass!

But in his picture in the mag he looked damned sharp . . . and . . . well, hell, maybe I'm cocky but I've kept *my* looks too. I'm one super-lookin' stud, and I got a big piece of meat—that's what they all want—if I just turn up one day, I reckon he wouldn't kick me out. Leastways, not til we balled. Once I get hold of him, no way he'll let me walk out!

Besides, I ain't got nowheres else to go.

Free again! Don't seem possible. Not that I'm gonna stay that way long if some asshole don't stop and pick me up . . . hitchin's against the law in this state. Hell, everything's against some fuckin' law . . . screwin' with guys is, too, so what difference does it make?

Keepin' my eyes peeled for copcars and jokers who might give me a lift took up the first few hours of my precious freedom. I'd been on the road maybe six-seven hours, had gotten two lifts. Was just about out of Ohio, headin' for Georgia which was where Rex baby lived . . . damn, is he gonna be surprised!

My notions of how I was gonna surprise Rex got interrupted by the sounds of a car brakin'. I hurried down the asphalt and got in

"Hi," I grinned at the dude. "Thanks for stoppin'. My name's Andy."

His name was Bob, he said. I figured he was lyin', he was as nervous as a cat tryin' to cover its shit on pavement. An older guy, not in bad shape, but he wasn't no ironpusher.

"Where are you going?" he asks me.

"Georgia," I answered. "A small town outside 'Lanta."

He nodded. "You're in luck. I'm going right through Atlanta. I can take you almost the entire distance."

I grinned at him, friendlylike. Maybe things were gonna work out for a change. Be the first fuckin' time!

What'n long before I found out you don't get nothing free. We hadn't gone twenty miles before his hands started feelin' up my leg, tentative, furtivelike (okay, okay! I learned the big words later!). I played along, what the hell. He had the car and I needed to cover a lotta miles, fast! He wanted to make it with me, fine! But he'd have to put out a little . . .

He was willin'. . .

I talked him into drivin' on til we nearly reached 'Lanta. Then we stopped for the night. He got us a motel room, one isolated, set off by itself. I didn't catch onto that part of it at first. Later, I figured out his reasonin'.

It was a wild night.

We undressed and I laid back on the bed, my big cockmeat half-hard, excitin' the bastard.

"Please," he muttered . . . "Stand up . . ."

I stood up, towerin' over him. He knelt down in front of me, makin' strange sounds, whimperin'-like. His hands, which were soft and womanlike, caressed my legs. Standin' like I was, my legs were rock-hard. His weakness kinda pissed me off. I had this picture of Rex in my head and what'n in no mood to do anything with this fucker. Only the fact I needed the ride got me in this situation . . .

My hand moved down to his head. I grabbed his hair, rough-like. Immediately he started moanin', beggin' me to hurt him . . .

"I shouldn't be here," he muttered. "Please, sir, whip me! Teach me how wrong this is!" His words, coupled with his unmanly hands, made me willin' . . . I grabbed him underneath his chin and slapped him 'cross the face, hard.

God, did he like that! Fuckin' bastard!

Minute I smacked him, his cock got hard—shot right up. I belted him a few more times, then suddenly he was sprawled across the floor and I had my belt in my hand, flailing away with it. His sounds only drove me harder. By the time I was finished with him, his ass was red and bucking, pleading for me to fill it. I tossed the belt aside and climbed on, ramming my dick up his fuckhole, not usin' no lubricant or nothing. He screamed at that, beggin' me to stop, but what'n no way I was gonna quit. The fucker deserved it . . .

By the time I shot my load in him, he'd stopped complainin'—was enjoyin' it! Leastways, he spurted all over the motel rug . . . afterwards, I cleaned up, got into one of the beds and fell asleep. When I woke the next morning, the cocksucker was gone . . .

At least he paid for the room. Even left me some money . . . for breakfast, the note said. Fuck him. I what'n that far from Rex's town. I shivered a little at what a fool I was, comin' this far with nothin' but a picture in my head.

But sometimes, I figured, you just had to take something on trust.

If you're ever gonna find anything worth hangin' onto, you just gotta start somewhere and trust a little bit . . .

Luck was on my side. I got three rides and by afternoon I was in the little town. I'd already figured if things didn't work out for some reason, I'd double back to 'Lanta and try gettin' established there. I'd always heard it was a good town . . . but something told me I wouldn't need to do that.

I had Rex's address . . . the asshole put it in that magazine. Dumb thing to do, but I what'n complainin' . . . I'd even figured out how I was gonna approach him.

Stoppin' off at a bookstore, I checked out a city map, found out how to get to his place and started out walkin' . . . what'n that far . . .

His place was neat . . . tidylike. I was nervous as hell walkin' up that driveway . . .

I knocked and *he* opened the door.

Stood there, lookin' like his picture, only better! He was workin' out, wearin' nothing but gym shorts and a lifter's belt.

"Yeah?" he asked, eyeing me. Torn, I found out later, between wantin' to get back to his liftin' and wantin' to make it with me at the same time.

"Hi! My name's Andy. I saw your name in that magazine. Since I was in town . . ."

His eyes lit up at that.

"Come in. As you can see, I'm doing my workout . . . hate to miss a session . . . but I daresay I might be able to forego it today. A different sort of exercising with a man like you might be fun . . ."

He always talks funny like that.

We went into his bedroom where he had his weightbench set up. He took off his belt and came over to me. I could smell his sweat. Never knew sweat could be so powerful. I what'n wearin' much, myself . . . pair of levis and a T-shirt. Rex reached out his hand and touched my chest.

"Nice . . ." he murmured. "What are you into?"

"Whatever turns you on," I said. "In the magazine, you wrote you wanted a dominant guy. Reckon I fit that bill."

"Maybe," he responded, "but you don't get me just for the asking. I want a man strong enough to *take* me!"

I what'n sure what the hell he meant by that, but I figured I was strong enough to take him down if I had to. I put my hand on his arm. He had nice biceps, and his pecs were rounded and tight. I saw his nipples were hard, so I pinched one of them, lightly at first, then real hard. He loved it. We were hittin' on the same wavelength. Our hands gripped each other's arms, grappling back and forth . . . he was one strong dude, but I was able to keep him off balance. After a couple of minutes we broke off and I pulled my T-shirt over my head and tossed it aside.

I watched him hungerin' after my body and for the first time felt like maybe things would work out . . . one thing was certain: he sure as hell wanted me. I could see that his meat was hard, projecting through his shorts. Fuck it. I unbuttoned my levis and was about to step out of 'em when he came over.

"Let me." His eyes stared into mine. I put my hand on his shoulder to force him to his knees in front of me. He wanted to be there, but he resisted . . . should'a known better. I slapped him 'cross the face. Next thing I knew, we were rollin' 'round on the floor. Wrestlin' hard, I finally straddled him, but he bucked so hard, he threw me off. I had to subdue him all over again. I was beginnin' to get annoyed. My hands, however, loved that contact with his sweatin' body. Finally I managed to catch him off guard and pulled his arm up behind his back.

"I oughtta break the motherfucker," I grunted.

He was still defiant.

"That the best you can do?"

"I reckon I got you stopped," I smiled down at his handsome face. "Now, muther, suck my cock!"

"I'll need both hands to get you out of those pants," he told me.

"You know who's in charge now?" I asked him. "You gonna behave?"

There was a subtle shift in his eyes. Something passed between us then . . . the kinda thing I've always wanted to feel, to see happenin' . . . A feelin' you wouldn't never have seen in the pen . . .

"Yes, sir!"

I let go his arm. Stood there, towerin' over him. Lovin' every minute of it, of him . . .

He had full dark lips, well-proportioned . . . I wanted them 'round my meat . . . wanted to slide my cock down that manthroat of his . . .

"Suck it," I grunted.

He undid my zipper and tugged my pants down 'round my ankles. His eyes lit up when he saw my shaft standin' ready for him. Throbbin', huge . . . hell, it oughtta be. It was all I had to give him.

His hands clasped my thighs and he placed those lips 'round my cockhead, rolling his tongue 'round the tip of the shaft, excitin' me, better'n any dude ever done before with just his mouth . . . I'm basically an ass man . . . and I figured he was, too. We'd get there . . .

And before I quite knew what he was doin', he pushed me back against the bed, so's I was sittin' down, and he had his face buried in my crotch, takin' that cock all the way to my balls, his tongue lickin' the hair 'round my sac . . . raisin' his eyes to see how I was likin' it, he withdrew his warmth from my meat, only to plunge back down the length of it again . . . I reckon I'd died and found heaven! Reachin' my hand down, I found his nipples and pinched them hard as I could, *real* hard . . . which only made him work his mouth harder . . . I moved my hands to his shoulders and pulled him up from my crotch to where we were facing each other . . . so we could fall on one another, eating the other's mouth in hot, lustful kisses, our tongues darting into unexplored cracks of each other. He had mirrors in the room, and as we lay there, I could see his firm, round ass in the air, lookin' like a gate to paradise . . .

His eyes caught mine.

"Want my ass, fucker?"

"Yeah . . . I'm gonna have it, too!"

"I know," he whispered. "I want to give it to you. Man, you're some hunk of meat. I want you on me, pushing that thick shaft into me . . ."

I closed his mouth by pressing mine against it. As we rolled recklessly 'round the bed, he reached up and grabbed a tube of lubricant. Somehow he managed to grease his ass and my cock while we rolled 'round like that . . . guess he's had a lot of experience, but what the hell, I what'n gonna complain. He finished his grease job, tossed the tube aside and poured himself against me. I could feel his heart thumpin' against his chest, sensed his excitement, his hunger . . . he *wanted* me inside him, in the worst sortta way—and that was just where I wanted to be. I pushed him to one side, swung my leg over his back and mounted him.

His ass was real tight. Always is, when a guy lifts. He gasped when I first pierced his tail, but lay beneath me while I slowly inched my shaft into him. God, he was hot that first time! I could feel him receivin' me, openin' up his crack, as he slowly moved beneath me like the first, hesitant rumblings of a volcano. He was hot as one. I ain't never fucked an ass like his before . . . I couldn't hold back, plunging my cock into him, drivin' it as deep as it would go, expectin' to hear him yell, not wantin' to hurt him —not like that. But he took it all, began movin' his body 'round my cock, squeezin' it with his ass muscle, drivin' me insane with lust. I lay there for a second with my shaft buried deep in his ass, my fuckin' balls restin' against the halves of his cheeks . . . then he began to back up into me, buckin' his body 'round, beggin' for all I could give him . . .

"Fuck me, bastard! You goddamn hunk of manflesh, fuck my ass! You're in me, let me *feel* that meat!"

Ridin' him was like bein' in the midst of a storm. I fucked him hard as I've ever rode a man, and he loved every minute of it. I got him up on his knees and pounded him hard enough to split most men in two. My hands grabbed his pecs, pinchin' his tits while he worked his own shaft . . . part of my mind was watchin' him in the mirror and registered the fact of his cum spurtin' from him like a geyser . . . just as I unloaded inside him. Knowin' he'd shot, I roughly pushed him forward and pounded his ass with my last ounce of strength as I filled him with my load.

We lay there, with him in my arms, our rasping breath gradually givin' way to normal sounds . . . our sweat mingled . . . he was some armful of man, alright. I was willin' to lay there forever . . .

Finally he broke the silence. "You're a *very* hot man, Andy. You going to be in town long?"

"Why?" I grinned at him. "Want a repeat performance?"

"I wouldn't *mind*," he stated. "You're exactly the sort of guy I was hoping might answer my ad."

"I could stay the night, if I was invited," I told him.

He invited me.

We didn't sleep much, though. I reckon by morning his ass was as sore as my cock, but we sure as hell had a session. Towards daybreak, however, when we finally fell asleep for real, curled up in each other's arms, I wondered how I was gonna tell him who I was and that I wanted to stay with him, permanentlike. Other than the fact we both was in good condition, we didn't seem to have much in common. He was educated, had a whole houseful of books, stuff I didn't know a damned thing about . . . well, I'd gotten my chance . . . he knew what I could do for him. If that what'n enough, reckon I was outta luck.

It was late when we got out of bed. He fixed a real fine breakfast, walkin' past me a lot, feelin' up my arms and chest . . .

"Hope you don't mind," he said. "I love to touch a man . . . especially when he's built like you . . ."

Hell, I didn't mind . . . except he kept my dick half-hard the whole time . . . fuckin' prick needed a rest . . .

While we was eatin', he said the right words . . .

"I sure wish you didn't have to leave . . ."

I looked at him.

"Reckon I don't . . . look, maybe I ain't been too honest with you, but I figured if you knew me . . ."

"Yes . . .?" His eyes were fearful now. Hard. What warmth he'd felt seemed gone.

"I'm Andy Parks," I confessed. "That guy what wrote you from the Ohio Pen a few weeks ago . . ."

I could see the fear . . . why the fuck couldn't I be lucky? Just once! He was plain scared.

"I wish you'd told me that before."

"Why?" I snarled the word, pissed. "Then you'd 'a been afraid I'd murder you in your fuckin' bed! Reckon I had *that* chance if'n it was what I'd 'a wanted to do." I eyed him. "I just — oh, fuck it!" I pushed myself away from the table.

"But why would you just turn up like this?" he asked, sounding really puzzled.

" 'Cause I hoped we'd get along good together. I kinda was taken with that fuckin' picture you stuck in the mag. Ad said you wanted a fuckin' *dominant* man! I figured if we got to make it, you'd maybe change your mind . . . give me a chance."

I turned to leave . . . what the fuck else could I do? "I just felt . . . maybe we could make it," I added weakly.

"Wait!" He barked the word. I stared back at him. I what'n gonna *plead* to stay! Not with nobody!

"I'll be afraid of you," he said. "No matter how good we are together, in the back of my mind, I'll always be wondering what you're up to . . ."

"Fuck it! Shit, man, I'm not gonna rip you off. Told you — I showed up 'cause from your picture, I just thought . . ."

Then he came up to me. He put his hand on my shoulder, looked into my eyes. And . . . told me I could stay!

# The Lure of the Sirens

He was the kind of man everyone despises—one of those nameless perverts who writes his phone number on public toilet walls or anyplace he figures it might get him some action. Every spare minute he possessed was spent in the endless search for sex; nameless sex, sex without love, emotion or sensitivity. He was abhorred by all. The kind of man parents warn their children about, one of those real sickos who hang out around public restrooms, waiting to service any willing male— old, fat, ugly, diseased, crippled or what have you. Anyone possessing a cock and balls was fair game. He was motor-mouth or a willing anus, whichever the situation demanded.

His lust was a never-ending thing. Never satiated, never done with. Rest areas along the highways, dingy piss-holes in the back of grimy arcades, all were his habitual hangouts.

Heterosexuals hated him with a mindless zeal, grateful to him nonetheless for reinforcing their mental images of queers. Homosexuals detested him for the harm he did their self-image. No matter how hard they worked upgrading their oppressed minority, there *he* was—behind every bush, every toilet, ruining all their efforts.

He might be any age or description. Mostly, however, he was fat, not very pleasant-looking and disliked by everyone he serviced. His sly, leering glances turned their stomachs, but the urges in their groins always allowed him his gratification. When it was over, men left him furtively, ashamed, embarrassed. If they passed him later on the street, their heads and eyes turned away so fast they were lucky they didn't suffer whiplash injuries.

He was thirty-five. Time's passage made him outrageously bold. Never arrested (at least not yet), he was forever flirting with phallic gods. The objects of his lust never looked at him while they were involved in these sordid little dramas. If any of them had deigned to notice him, and had been reasonably perceptive, they might have noticed his flashing eyes held a glint of hate and showed satisfaction at their mental anguish. There was little evidence denoting any sexual pleasure in the tableau.

When all was understood, sex was a long way from his mind.

He'd long ago given up much hope for sex. His humiliations were too great for that. Hell, how would *you* feel if every ad you read ended with the same litany: "Fats, fems and dopers need not apply." It was the only list he ever headed. Was it his fault his body never conformed to the slim, fashionable mystique the whole damned world was running after? He tried losing weight, God knows, he tried!

But what was the good of trying anything beneficial when nobody cared enough to notice the change? Walk into any place — a bar, bath, restaurant or whatever and watch the guarded flashes of hostility. Accusing stares, silently demanding to know what a person like himself was doing in *their* midst. Looks thrown so fast you almost missed them because no one wanted to be observed even *looking* at Fat Freddie. He grew thick-skinned in time. Learned not to show he cared, never let the dirty glances outwardly annoy him. He'd show the bastards! Wait until he lost sixty pounds and started lifting weight instead of carrying it around with him.

They were still waiting.

Underneath the blubber and loathing was a kind, sensitive soul yearning to be discovered and cultivated.

No gardeners ever came his way.

He lived in an unreal world, peopled by "studs" and "great-looking men." These were what he'd wanted when the dreams were young and fresh. The men then were like the dew — sparkling and alluring. But as time went by and he stayed the same, roly-poly, unloved, undesired, changes began taking place in his psyche. The subtleties of hate and disgust became tuned in him—he was a million-dollar stereo outfit, playing all the wrong songs. A country-western record on a disco-bar turntable. It wasn't enough simply to fellate a man anymore. Now Freddie wanted to be *sure* the man was ashamed, degraded by the involvement with such a fat pervert.

Freddie's pleasure did not necessarily come any longer from the piece of flesh in his mouth, but from the knowledge the owner of the penis was ashamed—was struggling between his own animal passions and his loathing for the human being who was relieving his lust. When passion and lust won out and Freddie was allowed to kneel before the man, he felt vindicated. He was dragging them down into the gutter where they'd forced him so long ago. Freddie knew they never viewed *him* as an individual person with his own dreams and desires. He was always something else. Something less than human, obviously. Because he was there, they used him. Well, being used could work both ways.

In the beginning things weren't supposed to be like this. In his youth Freddie thought love was supposed to have something to do with it all. Why he ever thought so is one of the mysteries of the age. Freddie was certainly never loved; a timid child, he was always ridiculed by his classmates, laughed at because he was so FAT. "Fatty can't catch the ball!" (Screw the goddamned ball, he always thought.) "Look at Freddie run! He BOUNCES! Fat Freddie is a sissy, a sissy!"

God! How he'd hated them! But at the same time, it should have been obvious he wasn't always going to be fat; one day he'd be smooth and hard in front, his stomach would go back where it belonged and would not obstruct the view of his feet—then he would find someone who'd like him, be friends with him.

He wanted to be loved so desperately! No one ever tried caring about him. His parents were as bad as the unpleasant playmates; no help from them. He grew up hoping for tender glances, a touch, a word, *anything*. He received nothing. The girls were

worse than the boys. As puberty arrived and deepened, they ignored him like everyone else.

Left alone, isolated, he became sullen, silent, hoping a quiet
demeanor would at least avert the periodic public unkindnesses.
It never did.

Sometimes Freddie couldn't help wondering *why* everyone
hated him so much. Sure, he was heavy, but his weight was only
a *surface* thing. Didn't *anything* else about a guy matter? Didn't
his soul or spirit or whatever the hell you called it have any
meaning to people out there? Apparently not. Disliking Freddie
was so easy, laughing at him so predictable. He was alternately
harassed and ignored; and of the two predicaments he never
quite figured out which he preferred. At least as they were strik-
ing him, pushing him into a patch of thorns or carrying him off to
be dumped into some mess of filth, they were *touching* him. He
was always starved for caresses — of any variety. He concentrated on their strong hands, the supple bodies and finally discovered he was what they called "queer." He often wondered if
he accepted the designation because they gave it to him. It was,
after all, the only thing anyone ever did for him. Yet with it, he
became a person, an entity, something with a meaning of its
own. Time enough later to see if he liked the application.

Anything concerning Freddie naturally was a put-down. He
soon found out being queer was even worse, if possible, than
simply being fat. And it wasn't true. He *wasn't* queer! And he
*didn't* do the things they accused him of doing.

His soul, of course, was pure. Snow-white pearls in a bucket
of coals. One day he'd look like they did! He'd be pals with
people just like his tormentors and they'd all say what a nice guy
he was, he'd fit in, be a part of things, part of the natural order.
Not different, not queer and not FAT! But incentive was needed
for any major changes in a person's character and the motivation wasn't there for Freddie. Or if it was, it got sidetracked.

His lonely youth grew into an even more dismal young adult-
hood. But not before his teenage years provided him his unique
brand of religion and a personal view of his new god.

Walking home alone late one afternoon, a winter evening,

darkness not far away, the streets nearly deserted, Freddie was surprised by a summons. Two classmates calling out from a wooded gully.

"Hey Freddie, come down here!"

A preemptory call. One with no modicum of warmth but not something in any case which might be ignored. Not by Freddie. He'd pay for it later if he disobeyed their call. The sirens sing so sweetly, it is said, they can seduce the wisest of men. Freddie in any case was never noted for his wisdom. He plodded down the terrain towards where they waited, managing not to disgrace himself by falling over his own feet.

The callers disappeared deeper into the brush, calling him again, enticing him. Ancient sirens, Freddie remembered, called Odysseus once.

Freddie, however, wasn't sensible enough to fill *his* ears with wax or restrain himself against the irresistible lure of his name on the lips of other people.

"Come on, Freddie, give us a blow-job!" They grinned at one another, snickering in the smart-alecky way of youth, not believing or caring that he really didn't know what they were talking about. Who'd ever talk sex with Freddie! Still, wasn't their call at least for *him*? Wasn't he finally being asked for something—in the capacity of himself?

"Come on, Freddie, suck me!"

He didn't want to, but the other youth behind him, at his side almost, was powerful, strong, pervasive. The speaker unzipped his pants and was standing ready. Hesitant, unsure, the act began.

Ugly, awkwardly at first, Freddie learned his trade. His eyes filled with tears over the humiliation but at least, for the briefest second, for one magical span of time, instead of being repulsed and hated, he was actually wanted. He felt human hands about his head, pulling him forward hard and energetically, against the flesh of another person. Later, he came to identify himself with those brief moments when the participants clutched and pulled at him in their agony of release, wanting in those flashes of time to penetrate him more deeply, saying by such actions

they needed him. Even the rejections which accompanied the
befores and afters could not negate those moments of need.

Freddie grew to love the small areas of naked flesh, white
usually, glistening and different. Almost a vision. A glimpse of
god, a god who chose Freddie as cupbearer, acolyte. He became
the anointed receptacle. Most of all, he became wanted. Needed
even. In those days there wasn't much stigma attached to a
blow-job from Fat Freddie.

Faith grows from small beginnings. Freddie often found himself backsliding, but god was insistent, never-ending in his demands. By the end of the year, Freddie became the only priest
(at least he felt he was the only one) of a new religion. One
which required constant sacrifices of him. More and more came
the calls, "Come on, Freddie . . ." and he responded with the joy
of a supplicant, the fervor of a true believer and the passion of a
bewildered teenager.

Yet as time passed he felt himself betrayed. The calls became
a mockery, the demons of his dreams called to him in the same
voices as the small bronze (thin) gods of his youth, and where at
first he worshiped later he slipped into apostasy.

What right did they have using him to obtain their goddamned
ejaculations? He began seeing himself as a person, a man, just
like those he'd believed divine. And like all betrayed lovers, he
plotted revenge.

He'd stay away. Let them flock to the toilets, the parks, the
rest areas. Nobody would find *him* there! The bastards could
use their hands, polluting themselves for a change. He was finished with all that! The loathing he felt at his actions filled him
with a ceaseless rage of hunger, yet no nourishment could ever
fill the hollow void in the pit of his vast stomach.

Tears were a natural part of his existence. Tears of outrage,
remorse, fear, longing . . . life should have held so much *more*!
Knowledge, however, brought no peace. Freddie found he could
not stay away from the rock to which the sirens lured him.
Having once heard the music of the deadly ladies, he was
drawn, irresistibly onward, by a mirage he fashioned exquisitely
out of his despair. Trapped by the fleeting hope of someday

being wanted, loved, desired, he fluttered hurriedly and awk-wardly to answer the new calls which came his way. No one bothered any longer to preface their slimy requests with his name. Now he was only offered a throbbing piece of meat, offered disdainfully in the full knowledge a creature like Freddie could not refuse, dared not refuse since he'd get nothing else. These impersonal gestures finally led to a basic change in Freddie's makeup. His confused mind tried to rationalize and build up an image of himself which would not reflect the realities of his life.

It was after this change that he came to resemble more the man everybody hated. The sly, leering toilet queer. As he aged, he sought a new maturity which might justify his existence and his activity. With age came renewed cynicism, the hatred of his encounters rather than the earlier adulation. The recognition of his life for exactly what it was, rather than what he'd hoped it would become. No longer did he dream of love—well, at least he didn't think about love in terms of sexual encounters; love was reserved for the quiet nights alone in bed, the proper place for dreams—he still wanted to service men, but now he resolved to do it on his own terms.

From this period stemmed his delight at making his subjects as uncomfortable as possible. Any raunchy remark, any un-wanted embrace or gesture he could get away with was given or made. Sometimes, of course, he was so obnoxious the trick left before Freddie finished. Those were the good days.

His program, however, was calculated to provoke confron-tations.

With maturity, the prospects of confrontations didn't bother him as much as they had in the past. He'd learned adults seldom resorted to violence as kids were prone to do—wasn't dignified for most of them. What married man wanted to be caught fight-ing a queer in a public toilet? Experience, too, taught old Fattie about how far he could go without endangering himself very much.

Yet for all his superficial knowledge, the whole madness was prone to miscalculations. Then, too, as the years passed Freddie inevitably made enemies. His foes were not, as one might suspect, heterosexual men, but homosexuals who vied with him for the use of the public places he frequented. The stalls behind the glory holes in the restrooms were prize strongholds, sought after and held, much like medieval castles. When Freddie held them, he annoyed everyone else—several nice-looking men, wanting these choice positions, were understandably disgusted whenever they found a troll like Freddie behind a partition.

"You fat bastard," they'd growl, "nobody wants *you*! Get the hell out of here!"

Freddie seldom availed himself of this advice and after a while the others would depart in fury, muttering angrily under their breaths. At one favorite spot Freddie was repeatedly warned to keep away—once he'd had water tossed all over him; one sonofabitch had even drawn a smiley face on Freddie's penis with an indelible pen—but of course he could no more abandon the place than he could have stopped breathing and still live. He was a modern-day Odysseus, determined to be the one who answered the siren's call—but without the precaution of restraints.

He waltzed into the place one afternoon. A quiet day. Peaceful. He'd had a run of bad luck at the rest area down the highway and was tense, nervous. In spite of everything he told himself, there was a certain physical need about his actions. No matter how shallow the encounters or how annoying their briefness, their anonymity, without them, he felt unfulfilled, in danger of losing his grip on his identity. He didn't admit this to himself, not ever. The mechanical obsessiveness with which he pursued his quarry did the admitting for him. He simply refused to acknowledge the fact.

When he was taut, before he'd knelt in front of his particular altar for the first time, Freddie was apt to act more rashly than usual. Today he saw the restroom was occupied by the two muscular queers who detested him.

"Hi fellas," Freddie spoke brightly, sarcastically, "waiting for me?"

"You better get the hell out of here." The words were delivered coldly, but intensely.

Freddie ignored the words as well as the hostility. "Sorry, it's a public john and I'm as much the public as you." He laughed. A tittering, feminine sound. "Maybe more, wouldn't you say?"

He wasn't prepared for the swiftness of their moves against him. One of the fellows kept watch by the door while his companion began pounding his fists into Freddie. Freddie, really surprised, began backing up, trying to escape. His foot slipped in a wet spot on the floor. He landed heavily on his fat, rubbery ass, hitting the concrete with a thud. The man above him continued raining blows onto the fallen man's face and body. The fighter was an expert boxer, while Freddie wasn't much of anything. He flailed about weakly with his flabby hands but made no progress towards bettering his position. Finally in desperation he simply placed his arms over his face and drew up into a fetal position and hoped his assailant would stop. The initial pain of the attack left a dull, throbbing ache over all of Freddie's oversized physique.

No intruder interrupted Freddie's thrashing. The only incident which momentarily relieved the pressure on the fat man took place shortly after he landed on the floor. The noise of the fight seemed to wake up an aged man who was dozing behind one of the partitions. He peered fearfully out of a peephole in the door of the stall and saw the battle in progress. Caution ought to have advised him to quietly remain behind the door of his sanctuary; he probably wasn't very wise. At any rate, in great trepidation he flung open the door and fled in sheer panic, leaping over the two men on the floor with the skill of an aging Nijinsky. The Cerebus at the door howled with laughter at the the old fellow's antics, while at the same time feeling considerable gratification over ridding the place of two such degenerates as Freddie and the old man.

The pair finally felt they'd inflicted enough abuse on Freddie. The fighter calmly washed his hands and combed his hair, not wishing to step out into public with his perfect features marred by any evidence of his handiwork. The men who followed him with their looks of inevitable longing would be disappointed if he were not perfectly turned out. While he was righting his appearance, his masculine friend ventured over to give the prone body on the floor a couple of kicks. Freddie grunted in fear and impotent rage but did nothing which might renew the intensity of the attack. The handsome pair sauntered out of the toilet, leaving Freddie wallowing on the floor in filth and blood.

The unnatural silence which settled over the place persuaded Freddie his agony was over for the time being. He feebly moved his arms from his head where they had grown tight and stiff from the violence of his grip and attempted to sit up. Unsteadily he gained his feet, staggered into one of the stalls and gratefully plopped down on the stool, banging home the bolt on the door. The blood from his wounds mixed liberally with the tears he was now shedding so profusely. He was a pathetic figure. After sitting there for several minutes feeling extremely sorry for himself, he unrolled a large sheaf of toilet paper and tried wiping his face. While he was doing this bit of cleaning up, he heard someone enter the place and creep into the next stall. Automatically his eyes went to the glory hole, and in another few seconds the object of his fascination came through the opening. Unmindful of the pain inflicted upon him, of his loosened teeth, and bloody mouth, he began his performance. He'd be damned if he'd let anyone run him out of here! By God! He belonged here . . . let those sonofabitches go somewhere else. Safely behind the locked door of the partition, Freddie heard the climactic music of the sirens and answered their call. He would always respond to the lure of the magical pricks coming at him in faceless anonymity. Nothing else mattered to him, least of all the man behind the meat.

# The Visitation

His face had that fresh-scrubbed look — like a Norman Rockwell kid grown up. His eyes were bright and cheery and he parted his lips in a half-smile showing just the right amount of perfectly-shaped teeth. I knew right away I was in for problems.

"Yes?" I queried in a chilly voice.

"I was wondering if I might talk with you for a few minutes?" he asked in a voice which was low-pitched, husky. The tone he used had all the right qualities of politeness and courtesy. Obviously a Jesus-freak. They came in all shapes and styles and it was hard as hell being rude to the bastards. Not that they minded taking up your time, oh no! Normally I'd shut the door in their faces, not liking their subject matter. Still, in some ways all of 'em were interesting folks — you had to have guts of a type to go up to a stranger's house and prattle about Jesus and God and all that stuff.

The main problem with every one of 'em — at least the ones I've run into — is they're all fanatics.

Now there's several ways you can handle a visitation from one of 'em. You can simply slam the door in their mugs and forget it, as I said already. But that isn't much fun for either one of you — they don't get their attempt at converting a downtrodden sinner, and you don't get the fun of making them mad. Of course, if you agree with 'em, well, that's another story and I'll let you take care of that one. As far as I'm concerned, they're generally a nuisance.

## The Visitation

Today was different. At least this guy had his timing right. I'd been out hoeing in the garden, wearing only a pair of cut-offs (my eternal effort at getting a tan) and was hot and sweaty. I'd just popped the top on a nice, cold can of beer when this self-appointed savior banged on my screen door. I had a few minutes, so what the hell. I thought I might as well see what he had to say for himself. Besides, he was all dressed up in a suit, looked uncomfortable as hell and had beads of sweat appearing on his forehead. But as I said, he was a pretty nice-looking guy. Clean, wholesome, All-American. Probably played football for his high school, looked capable of making a college team right now for that matter. He was, maybe, twenty-three.

So I answered him, "Sure, come in. Can I get you a beer?"

Now I know he didn't think much of the offer, but here I was being nice and friendly to him so he couldn't make a big deal about the beer. We sat down on my front porch, me with almost nothing on and him in his suit.

It's important as to who makes the first move in these conversations. Sort of like in chess, the opening player's supposed to have the advantage—at least if he's any good. It's the same way with a visitation. Since it was my house, I figured I'd start.

"You from around here?" I asked in an unoriginal, but helpful line of questioning. This would force him to start off telling me about himself and which church he was from. That way, I'd know what I was up against. The folks who do visitations come from several groups. Here in Georgia, you get some Southern Baptists, and they're bad enough, but they don't usually bother you at home. The street corner's more their style. Then there's these evangelical sects—used to call 'em Holy Rollers down where I come from—Pentecostals, Holiness, Adventists and whatnot. Lately the Mormons have been coming around. There's a few others—I can't remember 'em all—but the point is, it's good to start out knowing who you're dealing with.

"My name's Bob—" (They always give you their first name, but not the last—wonder why that is?) "—and I'm from across town. I and a lot of my friends at the new Mount Olive Holiness Church have been really having a wonderful time getting to know the Lord Jesus and we felt like sharing this happy experience with everyone. Jesus has really made a difference in my life and I know He could do the same for everyone if all knew Him. Are you saved? Do you know the Lord Jesus?"

Yep. Those two questions are usually the first things you get hit with. Most of these folks aren't very original. Of course the answers you can give 'em aren't all that great either. I'm always tempted to haul out that old bromide, saved from what?—but that's become a cliché anymore and besides they'll usually end up telling you, which puts you on the defensive rather than them. So I answered the second question and skipped the first. Sort of like with a government questionnaire.

"I'm afraid I don't know him—he died a bit before my time."

Now for heaven's sake don't grin when you're giving these smart-aleck answers. The whole point of talking to these people at all is so's you can watch 'em. This guy, like I told you, looked like an all-American kind of fella. If they find out right off the bat you're a scoffer, they'll pack it in and leave. The fun is in playing with them—especially watching their eyes. When they first arrive, their eyes are always sparkling real hopeful, like. If you try engaging them in an intellectual discussion about religion, their orbs usually become serious, earnest. The last stage, when they find out you're really only laughing at them, is when they get that cold, hateful fanatical look about themselves. That's what really scares the hell outta me. That's when I know for damned sure they're wishing we were back in the time of the Inquisition or the early days of this country when you got yourself knocked off if you said you didn't believe in all that stuff. And I'm not fooling—it *really* scares me! Damned Christians may talk about love and charity and brotherhood, but that's all it is—talk! The vast majority of 'em don't have any use for you if you don't agree with 'em. They'd like seeing people like me dead. Which I guess is why I enjoy baiting them now while I got the chance—I'm afraid in a few years, the way things are going, I'll be tossed in jail for such comments. You mark my words. Those days are coming back!

Anyway, this guy didn't like my answer, but since my face was perfectly straight, he accepted it as if he believed I meant what I said.

"Jesus didn't die," he assured me. "He arose again you know." (Always sounds like somebody getting up from a good night's sleep for a trip to the john.) "The Lord Jesus suffered death once so that we might have a second chance at eternal life."

"Damn!" I exclaimed, smacking my bare leg with my hand, "Missed him that time, too!"

Well, I could see that really pissed him off. His eyes took on a steely glint which told me what he thought of me. He was persistent, though—have to give him that. Most of 'em would have left after that crack.

He quickly moderated the hard look in his eyes. "I wish I could convince you that listening seriously to Jesus' message is the only sensible choice you can make if you know the true meaning of His ministry. Doesn't your future matter to you at all? I should think the idea of a whole eternity in hell would be so awful you'd stop and reflect about your life and where you'll spend the rest of it. Our time here on earth is but a moment of our existence, you know."

I gulped a few swallows of beer before taking up that one. He watched me drinking and I could see his thick neck muscles bulge and tighten with disciplined disgust.

"I suppose I might," I answered, "if I were convinced that there was an eternity to spend anywhere, or if I thought there was a hell either, which I don't. You folks are free to worship and believe whatever you please. I just wish you'd remember that other folks would like having the same rights."

"Rights aren't as important as winning souls for Christ," he replied gently.

That, of course, is the crux of their whole argument and the thing I can't stand about 'em. They make up their own definitions for the words and concepts they use. You don't have a thing to fight with except reason and logic and I never met a one who'd ever listen to anything as simple as reason and logic. The poor bastards *want* their beliefs to be true so damned bad they feel *anything* is justified if it will convince some poor stupid jerk into going along with 'em. Well, I obviously think the whole thing is a crock. Which, you might say, is my opinion and so what? Their belief's their own business and none of mine. Well, that's as may be. Here's one of 'em sitting on my own porch pestering me about my soul! He's not the first either, not by a long shot! Every couple of weeks I get somebody coming around trying to convert me. God! I sure must be sinful-looking! And I still say it's a hellava note when you gotta be rude to somebody to make 'em leave you alone.

And what about all these damned churches owning property and never paying a penny's worth of tax. That means I'm subsidizing them and I hate the thought of that like poison. And you can call me crazy if you like—but the day's coming in this country when all the old laws will be put back in force and unbelievers like myself will be lucky if we escape with our lives from these so-called "good" people.

Well, anyhow, we argued back and forth about man's rights and about souls and all that baloney. I have to admit the guy was tenacious. Most would have left already. But I shouldn't give the impression that *all* my remarks were calculated simply towards getting rid of the man, they weren't. Hell, I suppose I'm like him in some ways, I'd like to change his mind as much as he'd like changing mine. Not that I ever have, so far as I know. Changed anybody's mind that is.

So we talked on til I finished my beer. That's all the time I had to waste on this sort of crap. Gardens are demanding things and right now mine was crying for attention. These visitations are apt to go on and on. Especially if you try intellectualizing with the visitor. I've got a fairly foolproof scheme for getting rid of 'em, especially when they're young and good-looking as most of 'em are. (Seems like these churches never have any *ugly* people visiting.)

"You do much of this house to house evangelizing?" I asked, finally.

"I try getting out at least once a week," he answered. Then, "Why?"

"Oh I was just wondering if you might be back in this neighborhood again."

"Would you like me to stop by another time?" He asked the question in a real startled tone. I hadn't given him much hope so far.

"Sure," I said, grinning for the first time. "You're a real nice guy. I'd love seeing you again when I'm not so busy."

That unsettled him. More than all my comments about religion, that really grabbed him. But he didn't quite know how he should take it. Still, he was committed to saving the souls of poor sinners like me, so I suppose he felt obligated to keep trying if it looked like he had a chance of making any headway.

"You shouldn't play games with the Lord," he responded seriously. "I could pray with you right now. You needn't put off—"

"Oh, I'm not interested in praying with you," I said. "But you're something else, you know! A real great-looking stud like you! Umh!" (At this juncture you have to stare 'em right in the eye, very frank and hungry-looking.) "You come back when I've got more time—I'd love making it with you. I could *really* show you what loving is all—"

Naturally I didn't finish that sentence. As soon as he got the drift of my meaning, he was up and out of his chair saying goodbye. The funny thing is watching their eyes as the effect of what you're suggesting actually hits 'em. I've never yet had one come back.

I know, I know, you think maybe I oughtta be more sympathetic. Sympathetic, hell! And by God, you have to admit it's one way of getting rid of them.

# Masters of the Ceremony

The day was off to a piss-poor start. The ten-inch vibradong I ordered from a mail-order joint in 'Frisco arrived—busted. Really ticked me off as I was looking forward to playing around with it. You can figure out what sort of day it's going to be when your sextoys arrive and won't work!

I swallowed my disappointment and grabbed a hoe. There was work to do in the garden and I wanted to tend to that before the day got hot.

Now, my place is isolated (one of the reasons I need vibradongs). I'm located on an old dirt road, miles from the nearest town. Calm, peaceful, tranquil. The only drawback is lack of sexpartners, and usually I can put up with that. I'm a painter and where I live is conducive to my work. Two or three times a year, when I've finished a few canvases, I'll take 'em up to the big city—Atlanta—and indulge myself sexually. Mostly, though, I stay down here in the country. By myself, and content.

When I describe myself as isolated, that's what I mean. Used to be, maybe fifteen-twenty years ago, there were a lot of families living on this road. They're all gone now . . . the houses empty, most of 'em falling apart, except for mine. Other than the mail carrier, a whole day can drift along without any vehicles passing by.

So you could say I was kinda surprised when I saw this sharp-looking pickup rumble past. The driver was a black man, and his passenger, white, looked cute. Not being overly curious, I hoed away paying them no mind. The temperature got hotter; I took off my shirt. About an hour and a half later, the truck came back down the road, slowing as it neared my place, then stopped. The black guy got out. He was some man!

Around here, almost everybody is a racist or a liberal. I tend to be liberal—one reason I don't run 'round much in the community. This stud turned me on just looking at him. He was built on the order of "Mr. T" on the idiot box—exepting he had a trimmer body. Narrow waist, very broad shoulders and biceps all over the place. Damn!

*Goddamn! I wouldn't need no ten-inch vibradong if I could get my hands on that!*

I'm not normally so sexual-minded. But as I mentioned, it'd been a bad morning. The white guy wasn't hard to look at either. Short, maybe five-six, muscular, but with a servile air about himself. Here was a slave and his master if I ever saw one! What the hell they were doing in my neck of the woods was the mystery.

A mystery they soon dispelled.

"Hey man! Can we interrupt you a minute?" The black guy addressed me and held out his hand, tentatively. In this country most blacks never know how they'll be accepted.

"Sure," I told him. Them. "Getting too hot to work out here anyway. Come up on the porch."

They followed me up to the house and took chairs. I sat down and eyed my "guests."

The black stud had me *so* goddamned excited!

*He'd sure as hell be able to ram my ass better'n those two fucking flashlight batteries in that vibradong!*

I tossed out the thought and tried concentrating on what they were talking about. Paying attention was the hardest job I'd done in a week.

Their names were Rick and Wade. Wade was the black dude.

"We're planning on buying the place up the road," Wade told me, keeping an eye on me, to see how I'd take the news.. I wonder if my eyes lit up. Hope not. Around here, it doesn't pay to go getting eager.

We talked about their moving into the neighborhood. After half an hour, it appeared we had reached a point of, if not mutual trust, at least acceptance.

"The estate agent told us you might not take to company out this way," Rick said. One of the few times he was allowed to speak at all.

I laughed.

"I've got a reputation for being a recluse," I admitted. "Mostly I don't have time for idiots. I don't, generally, play the neighbor game. However," I added, not wanting to alienate this pair, "there's no reason to think you guys might not be absolutely *perfect* neighbors!"

*Whoa! Don't go overboard. Yet.*

"If you happen to need anything," I hurried on, "let me know."

Wade nodded. "We understand you, man. You'll find us *easy* to get along with. We do throw pretty wild parties, though . . . sometimes they tend to get loud."

*What the hell is that supposed to mean. Their place is over a mile up the road!*

I shrugged my shoulders. "You'd have to be loud as hell for me to hear anything. Out here in the country, racket tends to dissipate."

"Could be," Wade agreed, adding, "naturally, we'll invite you to one of 'em . . . but we've found our style of entertaining doesn't fit in too well with most local traditions. Of course if you're liberal-minded, you'd be welcome . . ."

The conversation gradually trailed off. At last Wade ordered Rick to follow him and they left. It had been an amiable meeting, but after they'd gone I couldn't rid myself of the impression they'd stopped by to prepare me for a hell of a lot of noise when they gave a "party." One they didn't want me attending.

Well, it wasn't any of my business. I figured I had *them* pegged. A master and his slave. The funny part was, they didn't know I played the same sort of games — at least, when it came to making it with guys. As for the other, I preferred things more or less equal.

As weeks passed, however, I found myself driving past their

place when I had to go to town. It was out of my way, but what the hell. Sometimes Wade would be working outside, no shirt on. Damn, but he was a big man! When that mail-order company finally sent me a vibradong—one that worked—I'd use it, picturing Wade in back of me . . .

In the country, time moves slowly. I didn't go out of my way getting to know the pair. We'd wave in passing. A couple of times they came by to borrow some implement. Once, I stopped by their place (at their invitation) for a beer and a look at what they were doing to the house they'd bought.

They obviously were paired up. I figured Wade was off limits. Rick wasn't my type and in any case I couldn't see creating a scene.

No doubt I'd have found a way to let them know we were on the same wave-length sooner or later. Fortunately, things came to a head faster than I dared hope.

About two months after they moved in, they decided to throw a party. I found out about it when large numbers of cars passed the house. They started arriving late Thursday. By Saturday morning, there must have been ten or twelve extra vehicles outside their place. I drove by around noon Saturday. Their whole front yard was littered with men. A lot of 'em were decked out in various leather gear. And they looked at me as I drove by (slowly, of course). Without bragging, I can state I'm a pretty hot-looking guy myself, so they stared. I suppose Wade and Rick had warned them about being *too* obvious if cars went by—and by and large, they were subtle enough—although if some of our fine Southern Baptist ladies had ventured past that afternoon, they'd all have had heart attacks!

Well, I hadn't been invited, so there wasn't anything I could do. Besides, Saturday is the only day of the week I bother with television. My favorite program—about this time traveler who zips around the universe in a police box—was on. I watched that and when it was over stepped out on the porch to peer at the night sky. A countryman's habit.

The noise from up the road *was* loud. Not music, although from time to time strains of that could be heard. I could have swore what I was hearing was screaming.

*Don't be an asshole!*

Fuck it! It was dark, and I knew the area like the back of my hand. It wouldn't hurt to take a peek.

The sky was crystal clear and the stars shone with a brilliance exhibited only in areas far from big cities.

I walked the mile or so feeling the sort of anticipation I normally experience when going to the bars in the city.

Nearing their house, however, I started.

They had posted guards!

And what guards! Two men, wearing cop-type hats, leather vests and dark trousers — whose material I couldn't make out — were standing at attention near the foot of the lane leading up to the building.

That pissed me off. Intrigued me. Maybe there *was* more to what they were doing than I thought. Drugs probably.

It was easy enough to slip round the back. Considering the size of the party, there was a paucity of lights visible. I crept past the rickety fence which bordered the back of the dwelling. Seeing the coast was clear, I carefully eased my way up to a side window.

Inside, the room was filled with men, most of whom were in various stages of undress. My cock hardened at the sight.

Three men were holding another spread-eagle on a board while a fourth was doing something to the guy's ass — inserting a fist it appeared to me.

It dawned on me this crowd might be *too* wild for me!

All I wanted was what I presumed to be Wade's big dick up my ass.

On another side of the room, various types of slings and harnesses had been installed. A man was being restrained in one of these in a manner which allowed other studs to work on his cock with their mouths. At the same time, behind him, a hooded figure was wielding a whip, lashing the dude's back. The captive jerked about as wildly as his restraints would permit. Whether from pain, pleasure, or both, I couldn't tell.

Could I possibly join the crowd? It was dark, even inside the house. If I knew this gang, they'd be so spaced out on something by this time, they wouldn't know (or care) who was who anyway. On the other hand, the whole scene was awfully *extreme*.

Reluctantly, I backed away from the window, ready to make my way back home. A huge hand suddenly grabbed my shoulder, scaring the hell out of me. The hand spun me around.

I found myself facing the dark, hulking form of Wade.

"It ain't very neighborly, spying like this, now is it?" he asked. His hand gripped me with a delicious ferocity.

Stung at allowing myself to be caught in a compromising position, I answered with some acerbity.

"It's not neighborly having a bash like this and keeping all these men to yourself," I snapped.

I could sense, rather than see, his grin in the darkness.

"That mean you're interested?" he wanted to know.

"I'm into guys, if that's what you're asking," I informed him. "Mostly, though, I prefer more . . . eh . . . less *creative* sorts of activities."

"Like what?" He hadn't released his grip in the slightest.

*Like your big black dick up my ass.*

I took too long manufacturing an answer. He spun me around and shoved me in the direction of the door.

"Me and my slave-boy wondered about you. Reckon you're feeling left out, ain't you? No need for that. We got enough to share—of everything!" His voice hardened. "Get your ass inside fella. How the hell did you get past the sentries?"

Our entrance caused a stir.

"Tom!" Wade called, "go get those fucking sentries. They let this queer get past 'em. They gotta be disciplined. Who wants 'em first?"

Several men spoke all at once. The two guards were soon flung into the room ahead of their captors. The scene began, to my way of thinking, to get out of hand. The erring sentries were hustled over to the wall and clamped into hanging pairs of chains, their arms stretched above them, their legs flat against the wall. A blond, nordic type, looking like a fucking Nazi SS officer to me, stepped out of the darkness and slapped the pair while muttering in a basic grade B movie dialogue that they would have to pay for their dereliction of duty.

Others surged round now and began ripping the clothes off the prisoners. The blond disappeared into a dim corner of the room and came back carrying a thin, dangerous-looking whip which he proceeded to use on the pair. Meanwhile, onlookers took turns sucking the erect cocks of the prisoners (how anyone could maintain an erection in spite of all that was happening to them, fascinated me). In the excitement of punishing the prisoners, I was forgotten by everyone except Wade and Rick.

Wade still had his huge hand on me.

"Want to play with us?" he whispered in my ear.

I shrugged my shoulders.*What the hell!*

"*You* excite me," I admitted. "But I wouldn't want to cause any problems between you two. And as for the rest, well, it looks a little too rough for me."

"How rough is too rough?" Wade asked, grunting his words in my ear.

"Why?" I asked, beginning to feel a sense of unease rise in the pit of my stomach.

By now Wade and Rock had propelled me away from the main crowd into an empty corner of another room.

Wade answered. "My little slave here has a hungering for your meat; as for me, well, from time to time I like more of a challenge than he offers. I got him trained *too* damned good. Sometimes I like to take a guy down and ram his ass, wrestle around some . . . maybe do a little fighting . . . before I rape his hole with my prick . . ."

*Now that was my kind of talk!*

"I wouldn't have any problems with *that*," I assured them.

"Trouble is," Wade went on, "when *we* get through with you tonight, some of the others'll want a turn. And Hans expects to perform the Ceremony later . . ."

Hans turned out to be the blond Nazi.

*What sort of Ceremony.*

I'd taken too long. Before I could *think*, and certainly before I was prepared to say "yes" or "no," Rick had fallen to his knees in front of me, unzipped my pants and drew forth my large, hard cock. His hot mouth around my meat, not to mention the period of time since I'd had a real man (as opposed to the vibradong) drove everything from my thoughts except the need to interact with the mountain of flesh by my side.

My silence was taken for consent.

Wade stepped in back of me and pulled one arm up behind my back. His other arm he placed across my throat. His mouth was next to my ear and I could feel his hot breath on my neck. I pushed my ass back into him and the bulk of his cock throbbed through the fabric of his pants.

He ordered Rick to undress me, which the little bastard did, quickly and efficiently. Wade *did* have him trained very well.

As soon as I was naked, Wade gave me a shove which sent me tumbling across the room. My foot caught on some discarded clothes and I fell to the floor with a thud. Before I could right myself, Wade was on top of me. His massive, black bulk pinned me beneath him. Dimly I realized things were far more serious than I'd thought. I exerted some strength of my own and our muscles strained and bulged and measured the abilities of each other. Had I concentrated on the wrestling, I might have been able to defeat him, for he'd apparently imbibed a bit during the night. As it was, all that flipped through my dirty little mind was how hard his flesh felt, how musky his scent, how like a raging bull he appeared to be.

Besides, every time I got a good hold on the bastard, Rick came over and attacked me, mostly by tickling me. Grossly unfair!

Wade finally mashed me into the carpet, lying on my back while his sweat flowed over me like honey.

He forced me onto my stomach and I sensed rather than felt him greasing his vast black cock. Then he slid down my body and plunged his meat into my hot, eager hole. I almost screamed at the sudden surge of pain. His largeness engulfed me, inflamed me — and as he slowly plunged in and out of my ass — enthralled me. The momentary pain fled, leaving in its place that delicious ecstasy of raw lust.

"Roll him over, Wade, please! Let me have more of his meat." Wade grunted, then jerked both me and himself to our knees: his arms reached around my chest and he fingered my erect nipples, pinching them with a violence I suddenly found desirable, necessary. Rick wiggled himself beneath my stomach and took my cock in his mouth.

Strange as it may seem, I never before had gotten involved with two men at once. Friends who had done so assured me that someone always got left out. As the three of us moved deeper and deeper into an abyss of flesh, we seemed to unite rather than separate. As our impetus towards climax grew, Rick urged Wade and myself into an upright kneeling position, and once we assumed the stance, he got in front of me and inserted my hard, wet cock up his ass. Wade then shoved us violently forward and I found myself in the middle of a human sandwich.

*Much* later, reflecting back on the night, I had to admit the position was too hot, uncomfortable and not exactly what I'd envisioned when I dreamed about Wade's dong up my tail.

During the actual operation, however, practical thoughts didn't intrude and I found myself fucking Rick's tight little bottom with the same enthusiasm I exhibited in bucking my own ass back into Wade.

It was all very surreal; certainly demeaning as hell. Happily, it was great fun! Fortunately, fucking leaves so little time for thoughts.

Our first time as a three-way we managed to do what we have seldom achieved since: erupt into a shattering climax at almost the same time. Wade's body increased its pounding action, as if he were trying, through me, to reach Rick's ass too. Not much was required of me, I simply went along for the ride as it were. And what a ride! However, the harder Wade's cock pierced my ass, the deeper he shoved my dick up Rick's hole. I felt my climax approaching and began furiously ramming the ass beneath me, conscious only of the exquisite physical sensations of our bodies melting into one strong male entity. Rick, somehow finding a way to masturbate himself, spurted his juice all over the carpet as the three of us fell into a heap of exhausted humanity.

As we lay there, I grew conscious of the fact we had acquired an audience. How long others had been standing in the shadows watching us, I had no idea. Slowly they advanced, in a circle, towards the center of the room where they surrounded us. There must have been ten or twelve naked men. All sizes and shapes, shadowy and ethereal in the dimness.

Wade rolled off me, grabbed my shoulders and whispered in my ear.

"You like my cock up your ass, white boy?"

My hand reached out, tentative, to touch his hard chest.

"Yes," I said. Adding "sir," as an afterthought.

He jerked my head around to face him. Could I see his eyes in the darkness? I don't know. Maybe it was the seriousness of his voice.

"Me and Rick, maybe we're kinda strange," he said. (An understatement if I ever heard one!) "But for us to make it twice — with *any* man — he has to be initiated into our circle. You got yourself in this tonight without being aware of what you were doing. I'm gonna give you one chance to change your mind."

"I don't know what you're talking about," I whispered, torn between listening to his words and watching the circle of advancing cocks in front of me.

Wade slapped me, then. Across the face, hard.

"Listen to me, man! You stay, you gotta take part in the Ceremony. Even I couldn't stop it, once we got started. I'm talking about pain, fella. *Real* pain!"

*That* got across to me!

"Are you *serious* about me not making it with you again without going through this Ceremony?" I asked.

"Yes."

"I want you again . . . but I'd like being aware of what I'd be getting into."

"No," he whispered. "You gotta agree *without* knowing."

I remembered something I'd read in a book. "Can you assure me I won't end up in the hospital or the morgue?" I queried brightly.

When he took a moment to think over his answer, I got uneasy.

"No way you'll end up in the morgue," he said finally. "You're too fine a piece of manflesh. The hospital—I doubt it. No one ever has."

I glanced at Rick, who was watching us (I think) intently.

"What happens to the three of us if I say yes," I wanted to know.

The sound of this Ceremony was beginning to make me feel creepy. Matters might have gone better had I possessed the foresight to ask the right questions. Unhappily for me, sex, as always, took precedence.

Rick eagerly reached for my cock, stroked my chest, and whispered his siren's song in my ear, "We'll make it as often as you want. As you and Wade want," he amended, remembering his training.

Wade held my chin in his hand and seemed serious.

"He's right, man. I'll plug your ass much as you want." He bent over my face and kissed me. Hard, passionately.

So I lightly shrugged my shoulders and said, "Yes."

*God in Heaven, was I a fool!*

*Or was I?*

Had I known what they had in mind, while also knowing the Ceremony was my key to participation in all the times I've found pleasure with this pair, would I have hesitated at taking part? Maybe not. But I sure as hell would have liked knowing what I was letting myself in for.

Which I didn't. Nothing in my life prepared me for the rest of that night.

First off, after I agreed to go along with the Ceremony, our attention returned to this circle of men who were slowly moving closer and closer to us. All of them were stroking their cocks and it was a hell of a sight. A dozen men pumping their meat . . . pressing forward against the three of us. As they neared Wade, Rick and myself, each man put his left arm around the man on *his* left. Each was using his right hand to pound his dick. A couple of 'em had *magnificent* cocks. One fellow in particular must have had at least twelve inches . . . as he stroked away, the shaft extended far beyond his hand. What a sight!

They pressed us into a tight area on the floor. As they towered over us, Rick moved his face into various crotches. I was eyeing the dude with the big dick, when he suddenly reached down and pulled my mouth towards his cock. I took as much of it as I could.

Their rhythm picked up, and a minute or two later as Wade, Rick and myself knelt at their feet, they climaxed all over us. Cum shot through the air landing on our bodies and on their bodies. As the cum flooded us, they grabbed one another, kissing and touching, while Rick and I pressed our faces into whatever crotches were in front of us.

Wade momentarily disappeared. I conveniently forgot his earlier words of warning.

Abruptly a light came on blinding all of us.

In the harsh glare, I almost giggled. The scene did have its humorous aspects—there were more than a dozen naked men all standing around in an otherwise (nearly) empty room.

My desire to laugh quickly evaporated.

The blond man strode into the room, glared at us and sneered. "Perverts!"

His eyes turned to me. Cold. Steel-like. He still had his whip with him and as the others moved aside he came to stand in front of me. Stopping about six feet away, he barked an order.

"Come here, whore!"

*Really! What had I done to attract attention to myself?*

I started to get up. His whip reached out and sliced into my flesh.

"Whore! *Crawl* to me. Avert your filthy eyes when you approach me!"

*Oh goody! Fun and games!*

I thought it all on the silly side, although my chest hurt like hell where he'd hit me. Still, I *had* agreed to play . . .

Submissively, I crawled over to where he stood, keeping my eyes cast down.

He was dressed head to toe in leather. His pants fit like a second skin and my eyes were not cast down so low that I couldn't see he was hung.

Once I knelt in front of him, I was unprepared for his violence. He raised his foot, placed it between my shoulderblades and shoved me onto the floor. His whip lashed my back, stinging, paralyzing me with pain to which I was unaccustomed.

I had to restrain myself to keep from leaping up and smashing his prettyboy looks.

He ordered four of the naked men to his side; they eagerly obeyed. At his command, they grabbed me by my arms and legs and carried me into the room we had abandoned—seemingly a long time ago.

There, I and the other two men we had left chained up were now strapped down on a curious apparatus.

It was a large board of some type. Rather like an incline board for doing sit-ups except that on this one, all three of us were spread-eagled, stomach down. There was enough support so that our heads could move. We could see what was happening to us in the mirrors which covered the wall we faced.

Holes were provided on the board so our genitals could dangle beneath us. Anyone who wanted to suck our cocks could have a free meal.

The only light in the room came from logs smoldering in the fireplace. As it was summer, and warm, I felt a better source of light might have been provided.

The show now became the three of us.

The three of us, plus Hans.

Wade had gone to the kitchen and fixed drinks. He offered them to myself and the other enslaved men. I gasped as I sucked up some of the liquid through a straw. Felt like he'd poured a whole bottle of booze into one glass.

"Drink it," he commanded, "you'll need it!"

*They're going to fist-fuck us!*

Since I've never gone in for fisting, the notion was *not* comforting.

But fisting wasn't what they had in mind . . . we might have been better off it that *had* been the scenario.

Hans positioned himself in back of us with his inevitable

whip. The way the mirrors were situated, we could see him in-
flicting pain upon our poor persons before the whip hit our
flesh. I was *not* thrilled by all these goings-on, but gritted my
teeth and tried not to yelp. My major mental activity was thinking that someday I'd get that blond son-of-a-bitch . . .

He practiced on us with his whip for some ten minutes. First
one then another. The room was strangely quiet, containing as
many men as it did. There was only the sound of the whip slash-
ing through the air, a sharp retort as it struck one after the other
of us. Finally, Hans appeared to become bored with the whip
and tossed it to an onlooker.

Moving aside, he announced arrogantly, "They are yours!"

His words brought forth noise, as the rest of the men cheered,
and quickly lined up in back of us. We got fucked, first by one
man then the next. In spite of myself, my cock hardened as one
stud after another mounted my ass, plunged his meat into me
then moved on. Those with an oral fixation moved around in
front and sucked our cocks.

Was *this* the Ceremony?

I had to admit, so far, it wasn't all that bad. Actually, I was
enjoying the hell out of it, in spite of the —theatrical?—aspect of
things.

Everyone finally had fucked us and cum in our asses as much
as they cared to. The room fell silent once more. Wade fed us
more booze. I daresay by this time I was somewhat drunk. Not so
much that I couldn't *feel*, just enough so that everything I *did*
feel, felt good! Some of the men sucking our cocks had also
drained us of piss. Nothing went to waste, apparently.

Suddenly Hans was back—marching up and down in back of
us.

"You fucking perverts! Whores! Letting men use you like
slaves! You're unworthy of being called men! Our society must
be protected from filth like yourselves. You must be marked that
we may know you for the filth you are! Each of you has carried
on as only a slimy, abject slave *would* act. Tonight those who
desire to own you will mark you as theirs! His personal property!
You shall be branded with the marks of ownership which

slaves like yourselves deserve!"

Three men stepped forward. Wade came up and stood behind me. His huge black body, still naked except for a pair of gloves, glistened in the flames of the firelight. The other two men stood behind each of the other prisoners. A dawning horror began to engulf me as I realized what they were planning.

We were going to be branded. *Actually* branded! The reason for the fire in the fireplace jolted my jumbled senses.

*This cannot be happening!*

My refusal to believe, however, didn't remove me from the chains which bound me. Men stood by the fire tending the branding irons . . .

I looked at Wade in the mirror.

"You aren't—" I began. Hans, furious, strode to my side, lashing out at me with his goddamn whip.

"Silence, whore! You cannot escape the punishment you deserve!"

Hans almost hissed. Were it not that the situation was beginning to take on a serious aspect, I'd have laughed. The son-of-a-bitch *was* good-looking . . . in a way. He looked as if he needed *his* ass fucked!

Unhappily, *I* was tied up at the moment, and *he* held that damned whip!

Finally the men at the fire nodded to the blond devil.

Hans turned to Wade and gave his benediction.

"They are yours! If you wish to possess them, mark them as your property! Brand them so others will recognize them for what they are—cocksuckers and sodomites, men who have abandoned themselves to lust and passion . . ."

He droned on and on. An *orator*, for God's sake! I didn't pay much attention to the rest of his words. Sweat broke out on my forehead and my belly started rumbling. I kept telling myself that they wouldn't actually brand us . . . right up 'til the time they did.

Hans, running out of words at last, strode over to a hanging cymbal. The men by the fire picked up the irons, the tips of which even a fool such as I could see were glowing red-hot.

They marched to where Wade and the others—(all wearing gloves, leather no doubt)—were waiting. Much like an olympic runner, they passed the glowing irons to those who waited. Hans struck his fucking gong and before I could think, the fiery tip of the iron was pressed against a tiny spot of flesh on my ass.

The pain was spectacular.

We were all so bound to the boards, however, we couldn't move our asses. The irons were held against our flesh for only a second—rather like a splatter of grease from a frying pan. No doubt the *thought* of the action was more painful than the branding itself, but you'd never get me to believe that.

The fucking bastards stood around cheering!

Wade undid my bonds and picked me up in his strong arms. My lips nuzzled his ears and I heard myself murmur . . . "You bastard! You damn well better be worth this!"

I felt his arms tighten round me.

"You'll find out," he promised. "But first off, this night ain't over yet."

*Oh Jesus! What NOW?*

He felt me tense up.

"Hey, relax! Now comes the good part. Leastways some of the guys think so," he explained. "The three of you branded in to-night's ceremony get Hans to yourselves . . . for as much of the rest of the night as you want. At heart, Hans is just a lady."

Wade was right, the blond bastard *was* a lady. With the memory of him and his whip fresh in our minds, we made quite a night of it.

## Grey Fox Books of Particular Interest

| | |
|---|---|
| John Coriolan | *Christy Dancing* |
| Margaret Cruikshank | *The Lesbian Path*<br>*New Lesbian Writing* |
| Daniel Curzon | *Human Warmth & Other Stories* |
| Patrick Franklin | *The Uncertainty of Strangers*<br>*& Other Stories* |
| Allen Ginsberg | *Gay Sunshine Interview* |
| Robert Glück | *Elements of a Coffee Service,*<br>*A Book of Stories* |
| Richard Hall | *Couplings, A Book of Stories*<br>*Letter from a Great-Uncle*<br>*& Other Stories*<br>*Three Plays for a Gay Theater* |
| Claude Hartland | *The Story of a Life* |
| Eric Rofes | *"I Thought People Like That Killed*<br>*Themselves"—Lesbians, Gay Men &*<br>*Suicide* |
| Michael Rumaker | *A Day and a Night at the Baths*<br>*My First Satyrnalia* |
| Samuel Steward | *Chapters from an Autobiography* |
| Roy F. Wood | *Restless Rednecks, Gay Tales from*<br>*the Changing South* |
| Allen Young | *Gays Under the Cuban Revolution* |